VOLUME 14   THE COMPUTER MUSIC AND DIGITAL AUDIO SERIES

Fundamentals of Digital Audio

Alan P. Kefauver

FUNDAMENTALS OF DIGITAL AUDIO

THE COMPUTER MUSIC AND DIGITAL AUDIO SERIES
John Strawn, Founding Editor
Christopher Yavelow, Series Editor

DIGITAL AUDIO SIGNAL PROCESSING
Edited by John Strawn

COMPOSERS AND THE COMPUTER
Edited by Curtis roads

DIGITAL AUDIO ENGINEERING
Edited by John Strawn

COMPUTER APPLICATIONS IN MUSIC: A BIBLIOGRAPHY
Deta S. Davis

THE COMPACT DISC HANDBOOK
Ken C. Pohlman

COMPUTERS AND MUSICAL STYLE
David Cope

MIDI: A COMPREHENSIVE INTRODUCTION
Joseph Rothstein
William Eldridge, *Volume Editor*

SYNTHESIZER PERFORMANCE AND REAL-TIME TECHNIQUES
Jeff Pressing
Chris Meyer, *Volume Editor*

MUSIC PROCESSING
Edited by Goffredo Haus

COMPUTER APPLICATIONS IN MUSIC:
A BIBLIOGRAPHY, SUPPLEMENT I
Deta S. Davis
Garrett Bowles, *Volume Editor*

GENERAL MIDI
Stanley Jungleib

EXPERIMENTS IN MUSICAL INTELLIGENCE
David Cope

KNOWLEDGE-BASED PROGRAMMING FOR MUSIC RESEARCH
John W. Schaffer and Deron McGee

FUNDAMENTALS OF DIGITAL AUDIO
Alan P. Kefauver

∎

Volume 14 • The Computer Music and Digital Audio Series

FUNDAMENTALS OF DIGITAL AUDIO

Alan P. Kefauver

■

A-R Editions, Inc.

Madison

Library of Congress Cataloging-in-Publication Data

Kefauver, Alan P.
    Fundamentals of digital audio / Alan P. Kefauver
        p.   cm. — (Computer music and digital audio series ; v. 14)
    Includes bibliographical references and index.
    ISBN 0-89579-405-5
    1. Sound — Recording and reproducing — Digital techniques.
I. Title   II. Series.
TK7881.4.K4323   1998
621.389′3—dc21   98-49181
                                              CIP

    A-R Editions, Inc., Madison, Wisconsin 53717-1903

    10 9 8 7 6 5 4 3 2 1

Contents

Preface

Digital audio is new and not new. The theories behind digital audio have been with us for some time. Charles Babbage, in 1842, proposed a system for storing and implementing calculations, and this probably would have been the first computer had it been completed. Thomas Edison invented a repeater for the telegraph of the day in 1877, and in 1928 H. Nyquist published *Certain Topics in Telegraph Transmission Theory,* which spelled out the sampling theorem much as we know it today. In 1943 the first computer, ENIAC, was developed by the U.S. Army, and the 1950s saw the publication of papers on error correction from Hamming and a redundancy coding scheme from Huffman. The 1960s were a time of development in Electronic Music technology at both Bell Labs and Princeton University, and Reed and Solomon developed a multiple error correction code that is still in use today. From then through the 1970s, work on digital audio systems escalated with the introduction of the Soundstream Digital System from Thomas Stockam and the introduction of the first in a series of digital audio video-based processors from Sony, known as the PCM-1600.

Today, digital audio is a fundamental part of our lives, and although everyone is not "sold" on the new technology, it is surely here to stay. These are the twilight years for analog audiotape, and as surely as the compact disc (CD) replaced the LP of yesteryear, digital audio workstations, CD recorders, and Digital Versatile Disc (DVD) machines are replacing and will continue to replace the analog reel-to-reel tape recorders that have been the workhorse of the professional audio industry for so long. In 1988 it was estimated that there were 100 million to 150 million CDs. In 1998 the estimate is that there are 500 million CD players and over 10 billion existing CDs.

Some time ago, a good friend sent me a copy of an article from a magazine called *The Gramophone*. The editor stated in the article that "the exaggeration of sibilants by the new method is abominable, and there is often a harshness which recalls the worst excesses of the past." As I read, I thought to myself that this was yet another of the digital naysayers who were prevalent during the earlier days of digital audio. Much to my surprise, when I reached the end of the piece, I found that this editorial was from 1925 and that the process the editor was referring to was the then-new electrical recording process introduced by RCA in 1924. Recent editorials have said similar things about the visual quality of the DVD. Seventy-four years from now, who knows what media we will be using for listening to music or watching moving pictures.

ONE

The Basics

■ SOUND AND VIBRATION

Sound has been discussed many times and in many ways in almost every book written about recording and the associated arts. Yet, without a thorough knowledge of the nature of sound, understanding how analog sound is handled and converted to and from the digital environment is impossible. Sound, by its nature, is illusive, and defining it in concise terms is not easy.

The Basic Characteristics of Sound

The major components of sound are frequency, amplitude, wavelength, and phase. Other components are velocity, envelope, and harmonic structure. Because we discuss sound as a wave later in this book, now may be a good time to visualize a sound wave in the air. Figure 1.1 shows a sound wave traveling through free space. At point a the source radiates a sound wave omnidirectionally away from itself. The sound energy from the sound source is transferred to the carrying medium (in this case air) as air compressions (point b) and rarefactions (point c). The air itself does not move, but the movement of individual air particles is transferred from one particle to the next in much the same way that waves move on the surface of the sea.

Figure 1.1   A sound source radiating into free space.

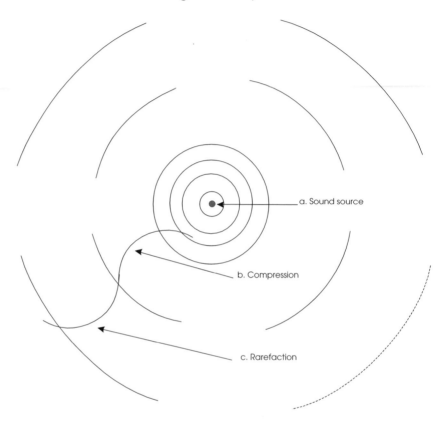

Velocity   The speed of energy transfer equals the *velocity* of sound in the described medium. The velocity of sound in air at sea level at 70 degrees Fahrenheit is 1,130 feet per second (expressed metrically as 344 meters per second). The velocity of sound depends on the medium through which the sound travels. For example, sound travels through steel at a velocity of about 16,500 feet per second. Even in air, the velocity of sound depends on the density of the medium. For example, as air temperature increases, air density drops, causing sound to travel faster. In fact, the velocity of sound in air rises about 1 foot per second for every degree the temperature rises. The formula for the velocity of sound in air is

$$V = 49 \sqrt{459.4 + {}^\circ F}$$

Note in figure 1.1 that as sound moves farther from its source, its waves become less spherical and more planar (longitudinal).

Wavelength The distance between successive compressions or rarefactions (i.e., the sound pressure level over and under the reference pressure) is the *wavelength* of the sound that is produced. Because we know the velocity of sound, it is easy to determine the *frequency* when the wavelength is known. The simple formula

$$\text{Wavelength} = \frac{\text{Velocity}}{\text{Frequency}}$$

can be changed to read

$$\text{Frequency} = \frac{\text{Velocity}}{\text{Wavelength}}$$

Therefore, if the distance from compression to compression is 2.58 feet, the frequency is 440 cycles per second, or 440 hertz (Hz). The period of the wave, or the time it takes for one complete wave to pass a given point, can be defined by the formula

$$\text{Period} = \frac{1}{\text{Frequency}}$$

Therefore, the period of this wave is $\frac{1}{440}$ of a second. As the period becomes shorter, the frequency becomes higher. This sound, with a frequency of 440Hz and a period of $\frac{1}{440}$ of a second, is referred to in musical terms as "A," that is, the A above middle C on the piano.

Musical Notation and Frequency It is beyond the scope of this book to teach the ability to read musical notation. However, this skill is essential to becoming a competent recording engineer, and the student is strongly advised to pursue the study of music if preparing for a career in the recording arts.

As mentioned above, the note A has a frequency of 440Hz (this is the note occupying the second space of the treble clef staff). The A that is located on the top line of the bass clef staff is an *octave* below 440Hz and has a frequency of 220Hz. An octave relationship is a doubling or halving of frequency. Figure 1.2 shows a musical scale with the corresponding frequencies.

Harmonic Content Very few waves are a pure tone (i.e., a tone with no additional harmonic content). In fact, only a sine wave is a true pure tone. When an object (e.g., a bell) is struck, several tones at different frequencies

Figure 1.2 A musical scale.

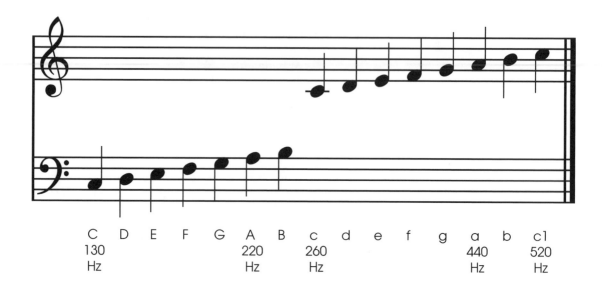

are produced. The fundamental resonance tone of the bell is heard first, followed by other frequencies at varying amplitudes. The next tone is a doubling of the fundamental frequency (an octave) above that, followed by another doubling that is heard as a musical interval of a fifth.

For example, a bell with a fundamental frequency of 64Hz produces harmonics of 128Hz and 192Hz, which is a G, a fifth above the second C. Many other harmonics at varying amplitudes are produced, depending on the metallic composition of the bell. These harmonics are arranged in a relationship called the *overtone series,* and the combination of these harmonies, or *overtones,* gives sound its specific *timbre,* or tone coloration.

The difference in harmonic content makes an oboe sound different from a clarinet. Although an oboe and a clarinet produce the same note with the same fundamental frequency, the number of overtones and the amplitude of each differs.

The overtone series is most often notated in the musical terminology of octaves, fifths, fourths, and so on but actually corresponds to the addition of the fundamental frequency. Therefore, an overtone series based on the note C is, in hertz, 65, 130, 195, 260, 325, 390, 455, 520, 585, 650, 715, and so on. In musical terms this is a

Figure 1.3   The musical overtone series.

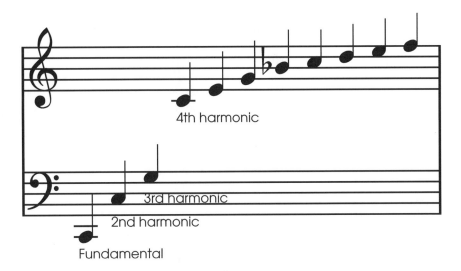

4th harmonic

3rd harmonic

2nd harmonic

Fundamental

series of the fundamental followed by an octave, a perfect fifth, a perfect fourth, a major third, a minor third, another minor third, three major seconds, and a minor second (see figure 1.3). The frequency that is twice the frequency of the fundamental is called the *second harmonic* even though it is the first overtone. Confusion often exists concerning this difference in terminology.

The third harmonic is the first non-octave relationship above the fundamental (it is the fifth), and as such any distortion in this harmonic tone is often detected before distortion is heard in the tone a fifth below (the second harmonic). Many audio products list the percentage of third harmonic distortion found (because it is the most audible) as part of their specifications.

The Sound Envelope   All sounds have a start and an end. A drop in amplitude, called a *decay,* often occurs after the start of the sound and is followed by a sustain and a final drop in amplitude before the event ends completely. The four main parts of the *sound envelope* are (1) the attack,

(2) the initial decay, (3) the sustain (or internal dynamic), and (4) the final decay (often referred to as the *release*). These are shown in figure 1.4.

The *attack* is the time that it takes for the sound generator to respond to whatever has set it into vibration. Different materials, with their different masses, have different attack times. How an object is set into vibration also affects its attack time. A softly blown flute has a longer attack time than a sharply struck snare drum. In general, struck instruments have an attack time that is much faster (in the 1- to 20-millisecond range) than wind instruments (in the 60- to 200-millisecond range). String attack times vary, depending on whether the instrument is bowed or plucked. The attack time of an instrument can be represented by an equivalent frequency based on the following formula:

$$\Delta T = \frac{1}{Frequency}$$

Rearranging this formula gives

$$Frequency = \frac{1}{\Delta T}$$

Figure 1.4   The envelope of an audio signal.

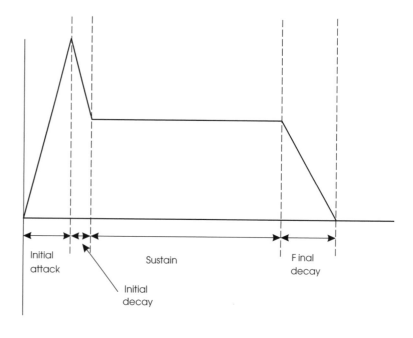

This means that if an instrument has an attack time of 1 millisecond, the equivalent frequency is 1 kilohertz (kHz). This is an important fact to remember when trying to emphasize the attack of an instrument. The prudent engineer remembers this when applying equalization, or tonal change, to a signal.

The *initial decay,* which occurs immediately after the attack on most instruments, is caused by the cessation of the force that set the tube, string, or medium into vibration. The length of the *sustain* varies, depending on whether the note is held by the player for a specific period of time (e.g., when a trumpet player holds a whole note) or on how long the medium continues to vibrate (medium resonance) before beginning the *final decay,* which occurs when the sound is no longer produced by the player or by the resonance of the vibrating medium. As the trumpet player releases a held note, the air column in the instrument ceases to vibrate, and the amplitude decays exponentially until it is no longer audible. Final decays vary from as short as 250 milliseconds to as long as 100 seconds, depending on the vibrating medium. However, not all frequencies or harmonics decay at the same rate. Most often, the high-frequency components of the sound decay faster than the low-frequency ones. This causes a change in the sound's timbre and helps define the overall sound of the instrument (or other sound-producing device).

Masking Many references can be found in the literature about the equal loudness contours (discussed later in this chapter) developed by Fletcher and Munson and later updated by Robinson and Dadson. These curves relate our perception of loudness at varying frequencies and amplitudes and apply principally to single tones. How many times have you sat in a concert hall listening to a recital in which one instrumentalist drowned out another? Probably more than once. When you consider the fact that a piano, even at half-stick (i.e., with the lid only partially raised), can produce a level of around 6 watts, whereas a violinist, at best, produces 6 milliwatts, it is easy to understand why the violinist cannot be heard all the time. Simply stated, loud sounds *mask* soft ones. The masking sound needs to be only about 6 decibels higher than the sound we want to hear to mask the desired sound.

It makes perfect sense that a loud instrument will cover a softer one if they are playing the same note or tone, but what if one instrument is playing a C and another an A? Studies by Zwicker and Feldtkeller have shown that even a narrow band of noise can mask a tone that is not included in the spectrum of the noise itself. For example, a low-frequency sine wave can easily mask, or apparently reduce the level of, a higher sinusoidal note that is being sounded at the same time. This masking occurs within the basilar structure of the ear itself. The louder tone causes a loss in sensitivity in neighboring sections of the basilar membrane. The greatest amount of masking occurs above the frequency of the masking signal rather than below it, and the greater the amplitude of the masking signal, the wider the frequency range masked.

However, when a note is produced by an instrument that has a complicated, dense sound spectrum (i.e., a note with a rich harmonic structure), that sound will usually mask sounds that are less complicated (less dense). In fact, many newer buildings that use modular, or "carrel," types of office space are equipped to send constant low-level random wide-band noise through loudspeakers in their ceilings. This masking signal keeps the conversations in one office carrel from intruding into adjacent office space. The level of the masking signal is usually around 45 decibels, and this (plus the inverse square law, which is discussed later) effectively provides speech privacy among adjacent spaces. This effect is used also by some noise reduction systems when, as the signal rises above a set threshold, processing action is reduced or eliminated. In addition, the masking effect is a critical part of the data-reduction systems used in some of the digital audio storage systems discussed later in this book.

Localization

It is a fact that a person with one ear can perceive pitch, amplitude, envelope, and harmonic content but cannot determine the direction from which the sound originates. The ability to localize a sound source depends on using both ears, often referred to as *binaural hearing*. Several factors are involved in binaural hearing, depending on the frequency of the sound being perceived.

The ears are separated by a distance of about $6\frac{1}{2}$ or 7 inches so that sound waves diffract around the head to reach both ears. When the wavelength of sound is long, the diffraction effect is minimal and the comparative amplitude at each ear about the same. However, when the wavelength is short, the diffraction effect is greater and the sound attenuated at the farther ear. Because the sound has to travel farther relative to wavelength, there is a perceptual time difference factor as well. You may have noticed that it is easier to locate high-frequency sounds than low-frequency ones. In fact, low-frequency signals often appear to be omnidirectional because of this effect. We can say that high frequencies (above 1kHz) are localized principally by amplitude and time differences between the two ears.

How, then, do we localize low frequencies? With all sound there is a measurable time-of-arrival difference between the two ears when the sound is to one side or the other. As the sound moves to a point where it is equidistant from both ears, these time differences are minimized. With longer wavelengths the time-of-arrival differences are less noticeable because the ratio of the time difference to the period of the wave is large. However, this creates phase differences between the two ears, allowing the brain to compute the relative direction of the sound. Therefore, we can say that low frequencies are located by intensity and phase differences.

The Haas Effect and the Inverse Square Law

Although much has been said and written about the Haas effect, also known as the precedence effect, and the inverse square law, we can say that the sound we hear first defines for us the apparent source of the sound. Consider the following example. Two trumpet players stand in front of you, one slightly to the right at a distance of 5 feet and another slightly to the left at a distance of 10 feet. If they play the same note at the same amplitude, you will localize the sound to the right because it is louder. This amplitude difference is due to the *inverse square law,* which states that for every doubling of distance there is a 6-decibel loss in amplitude in free space (i.e., where there are no nearby reflecting surfaces). Now suppose that both players sustain their notes. If player A (on the left) increases his amplitude by 6 decibels, the sound levels will balance, but your ear-brain combination will insist that player B (on the right) is closer to you than player A. Although the levels have been equalized, you perceive the nearer player to be closer. Why? You would think that as long as the levels are identical at both ears, the players would appear to be equidistant from you.

According to Haas, "Our hearing mechanism integrates the sound intensities over short time intervals similar, as it were, to a ballistic measuring instrument." This means that the ear-brain combination integrates the very short time differences between the two ears, causing the sound with the shortest timing differences to appear louder and therefore closer. Haas used two sound sources and, while delaying one, asked a subject to vary the loudness of the other source until it matched the sound level of the delayed sound. He found that where the delay was greater than 5 but less than 30 milliseconds, the amplitude of the delayed source had to be 10 decibels louder than the signal from the nondelayed source for the two sounds to be perceived as equal. Beyond a delay of 30 milliseconds a discrete echo was perceived, and prior to 5 milliseconds the level needed to be increased incrementally as the delay lengthened.

■ THE DECIBEL

Earlier in this chapter we discussed the basic characteristics of sound, but one that was conspicuously absent was *amplitude*. The unit of measure that is normally used to define the amplitude of sound levels is the *decibel* (dB). A *Bel* is a large, rather cumbersome unit of measure, so for convenience it is divided into 10 equal parts and prefaced with *deci* to signify the one-tenth relationship. Therefore, a decibel is one tenth of a Bel.

A sound level meter measures sound in the environment. A large commercial aircraft taking off can easily exceed 130dB, whereas a quiet spot in the summer woods can be a tranquil 30dB. Most good sound level meters are capable of measuring in the range of 0dB to 140dB. You might think that the 0dB level is the total absence of sound, but it is not. Actually, 0dB is the lowest sound pressure level that an average listener with normal hearing can perceive. This is called the *threshold of hearing*. The 0dB reference level corresponds to a sound pressure level of 0.00002 dynes per square centimeter (dynes/cm^2), which, referenced to power or intensity in watts, equals 0.000000000001 watts per square meter (W/m^2). Also referred to in this book is the threshold of feeling, which is typically measured as an intensity of 1W/m^2. A typical professional sound level meter is shown in figure 1.5.

As you can see, the decibel must have a reference, which, when we discuss sound levels in an acoustic environment, is the threshold of hearing. In fact, the decibel is defined as 10 times the logarithmic relationship between two powers. The formula for deriving the decibel is

$$dB = 10\log\left(\frac{\text{Power}_A}{\text{Power}_B}\right)$$

where Power$_A$ is the measured power and Power$_B$ the reference power. We can use this formula to define the amplitude range of human hearing by substituting the threshold of hearing (0.000000000001W/m^2) for the reference power and using the

Figure 1.5   A professional sound level meter (courtesy B and K Corporation).

threshold of feeling (1W/m^2) as the measured power. The formula, with the proper values plugged in, looks like this:

$$10\log \frac{1\text{W/m}^2}{1 \times 10^{-12}\ \text{W/m}^2} = 120\text{dB}$$

Therefore, the dynamic range of the human ear is 120dB. Figure 1.6 shows typical sound pressure levels, related to the threshold of hearing, found in our everyday environment. Note also the level called the *threshold of pain.*

It is interesting to note that other values that can be obtained using the power formula. For example, if we use a value of 2W in the measured power spot and a value of 1W in the reference power spot, we find that the result is 3dB. That is, any 2-to-1 power relationship can be defined simply as an increase in level of 3dB. Whether the increase in power is from 100W to 200W or from 2,000W to 4,000W, the increase in level is still 3dB.

Figure 1.6   Typical sound pressure levels in decibels.

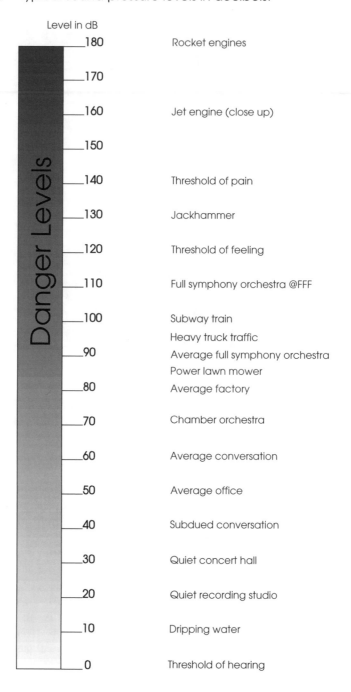

The inverse square law was mentioned earlier in this chapter. You might surmise that doubling distance would cause a sound level loss of one half, or -3dB. However, you must remember that sound radiates omnidirectionally from the source of the sound. Recall from your high school physics class that the area of a sphere is determined by the formula a $4\pi r^2$. It follows that when a source radiates to a point that is double the distance from the first, it radiates into four times the area instead of twice the area. This causes a 6dB loss of level instead of a 3dB one. The formula for the inverse square law is

$$\text{Level drop} = 10\log\left(\frac{r^2}{r^1}\right)^2 = 20\log\left(\frac{r^2}{r^1}\right) = 6\text{dB}$$

where r^1 equals 2 feet and r^2 equals 4 feet. Figure 1.7 shows this phenomenon. Note that at a distance of 2 feet, the sound pressure level

Figure 1.7   The inverse square law.

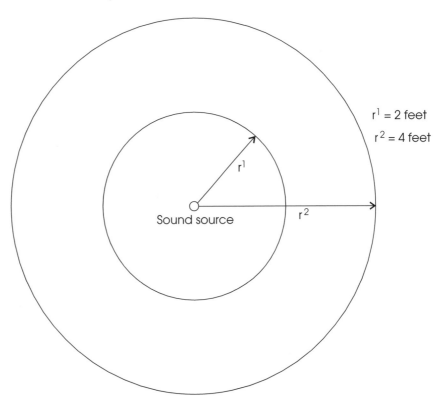

$r^1 = 2$ feet

$r^2 = 4$ feet

Sound source

is 100dB. When the listener moves to a distance of 4 feet (i.e., twice the original distance), the level drops to 94dB.

Equal Loudness Contours

Ambient, or background, noise is all around us. Even in a quiet concert hall, the movement of air in the room can be 30dB or more above the threshold of hearing at one or more frequencies. However, the ear is not equally sensitive to sound pressure at all frequencies.

The ear is most sensitive to the frequency range between 3,000Hz and 5,000Hz. A tone that is heard just at the threshold of hearing $(1 \times 10^{-12}W/m^2)$ at a frequency of 4,000Hz corresponds to a sound pressure level of 0dB. For the tone to be perceived by the same listener at the same loudness level when the frequency is lowered to 400Hz, the amplitude of the tone must be raised about 12dB. If we lower the frequency to 40Hz, the level must be raised nearly 45dB to be perceived at the same volume. Figure 1.8 shows the equal loudness contours developed by Fletcher and Munson and updated later by Robinson and Dadson.

The contours are labeled *phons,* which range from 10 to 120; at 1,000Hz the phon level is the same as the sound pressure level in decibels. Therefore, the phon is a measure of equal loudness. Figure 1.8 has a curve labeled "MAF," which stands for "minimum audible field." This curve, equal to 0 phons, defines the threshold of hearing. Note that at low sound pressure levels, low frequencies must be raised substantially in level to be perceived at the same loudness as 1kHz. Frequencies above 5kHz (5,000Hz) need to be raised as well, although not as much. Looking at figure 1.8, you can see that the discrepancies between lows, highs, and mid tones are reduced as the level of loudness increases. The 90-phon curve shows a variation of 40dB, whereas the 20-phon curve shows one of nearly 70dB.

The sound level meter in figure 1.5 has several weighting networks so that at different sound pressure levels the meter can better approximate the response of the human ear. The A, B, and C weighting networks correspond to the 40-, 70-, and 100-phon curves of the equal loudness contours.

Logarithms

As you may have noticed, the formula used to define the decibel applied *logarithms,* abbreviated "log." Anyone involved in the audio engineering process needs to understand logarithms. In brief, a logarithm of a number is that power to which 10 must be raised to equal that number—not multiplied but raised. The shorthand notation for

Figure 1.8   The Robinson-Dadson equal loudness contours.

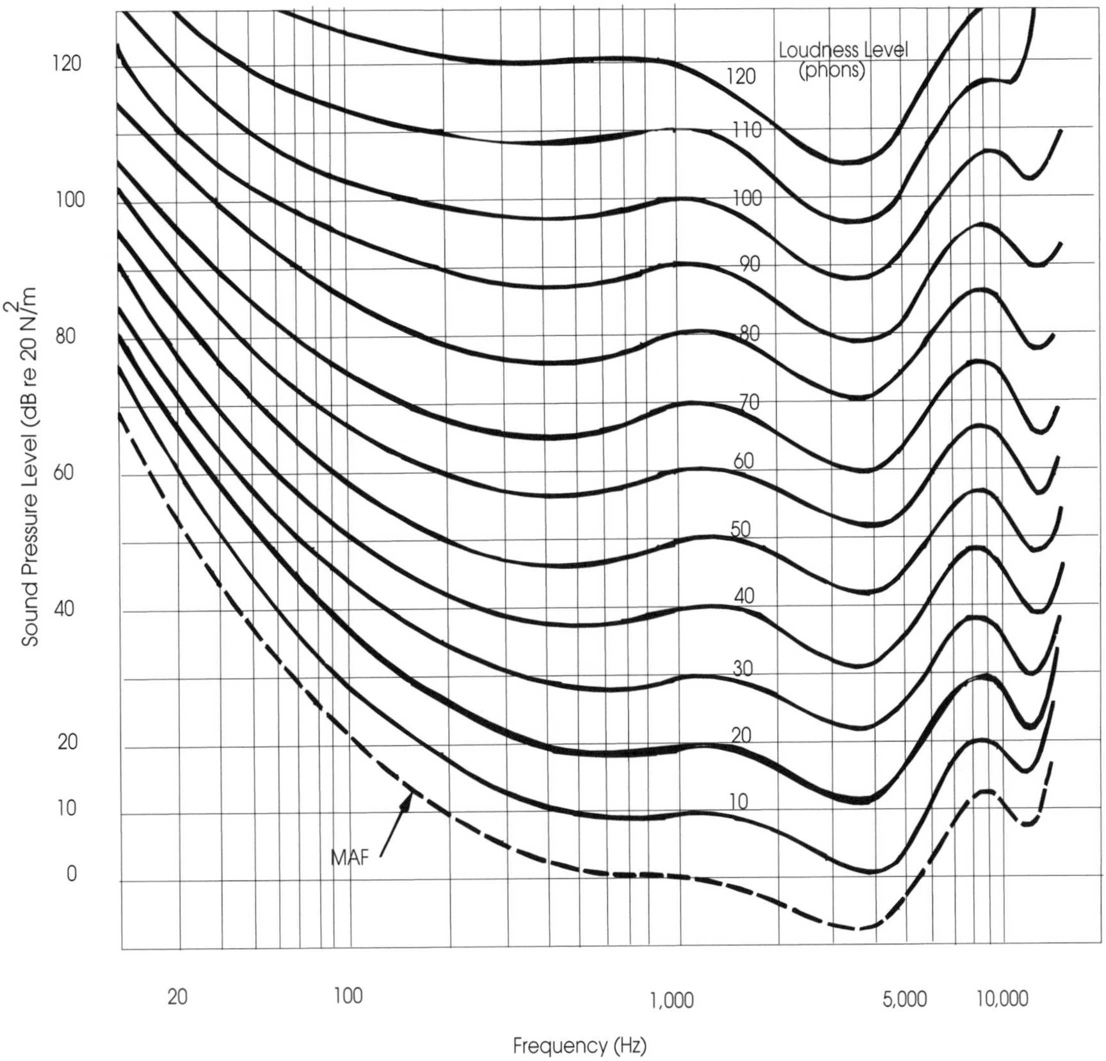

this is 10^x, where x, the *exponent*, indicates how many times the number is to be multiplied by 10. Therefore, 10^3 is 10 raised to the third power, or simply "10 to the third":

$$10^1 = 10$$
$$10^2 = 100$$
$$10^3 = 1,000$$
$$10^9 = 1,000,000,000$$

Numbers whose value is less than 1 can be represented with negative exponents, such as

$$0.1 = 10^{-1}$$
$$0.01 = 10^{-2}$$
$$0.001 = 10^{-3}$$
$$0.000001 = 10^{-6}$$

Because we are talking about very large and very small numbers, prefix names can be added to terms such as *hertz* (frequency) and *ampere* (a measure of current flow) to indicate these exponents. Therefore, for large numbers,

1,000 cycles per second = 10^3 hertz (or 1 kilohertz [1kHz])
10^6 hertz = 1 megahertz or (1MHz)
10^9 hertz = 1 gigahertz (1GHz)
10^{12} hertz = 1 terahertz (1THz)

For small numbers,

0.001 ampere (A) = 10^{-3} A (or 1 milliamp [1mA])
10^{-6} A = 1 microamp (1µA)
10^{-9} = 1 nanoamp (1nA)
10^{-12} A = 1 picoamp (1pA)

Now you can see that the threshold of hearing, defined earlier as $0.000000000000\text{W/m}^2$, appears in the formula as $1 \times 10^{-12}\text{W/m}^2$. It is also helpful to know that when powers of 10 are multiplied or divided, you simply add or subtract the exponents. Therefore, $10^6 \times 10^3 = 10^{6+3} = 10^9$, and $10^{12} \div 10^9 = 10^{12-9} = 10^3$. Logarithms of numbers also exist between, for example, 1 and 10 and 10 and 100, but we will leave those problems to the mathematicians. Today, the logarithm of any number can easily be found by either looking them up in a table or pushing the log button on a calculator.

Reference Levels and Metering

When we discuss reference levels, we are talking about the values of the current and voltage that pass through a cable between two pieces of equipment. *Ohm's law* establishes some fundamental relationships that we should be aware of. Power, expressed in watts, is equal to either the square of the voltage divided by the resistance or the square of the current multiplied by the resistance in the circuit, that is, $P = E^2/R$ and $P = I^2R$, respectively. In professional audio circuits we work with voltage levels instead of power levels, and because the resistance in the circuit is constant, we do not need to be concerned with R at this time. To calculate the difference between two powers, we use the power formula:

$$dB = 10\log\left(\frac{Power_A}{Power_B}\right)$$

Because we really want to know the decibel level referenced to volts, the formula should read

$$dB = 10\log\left(\frac{E_A^2}{E_B^2}\right)$$

To remove the squares from the voltages in the formula we can rewrite the expression as

$$dB = 20\log\left(\frac{E_A}{E_B}\right)$$

Note now that any 2-to-1 voltage relationship will yield a 6dB change in level instead of the 3dB change of the straight power formula.

There is always a standard *reference level* in audio circuits. This reference level, an electrical zero reference, is equivalent to the voltage found across a common resistance in the circuit. Therefore, we can compare levels by noting how many decibels the signal is above or below the reference level.

The dBm   The standard professional audio reference level is +4dBm. The dBm is a reference level in decibels relative to 1 milliwatt (mW). Zero dBm is actually the voltage drop across a 600-ohm resistor in which 1mW of power is dissipated. Using Ohm's law ($P = E^2/R$) we find that the voltage is 0.775 volts RMS. (This value is merely a convenient reference point and has no intrinsic significance.) The meters that were used on the original audio circuits when this standard was enacted were vacuum tube volt meters (VTVMs). As the demand for more meters grew (as stereo moved to multitrack), a less expensive meter was needed. An accurate meter, which needs a low impedance, would load down the circuit it was measuring and thereby cause false readings. To compensate for the loading effect of the meter, a 3.6KΩ resistor was inserted in the meter path. Now the meter no longer affected the circuit it was measuring, although it read 4dBm lower. When the meter was raised to 0VU (volume units), the actual line level was +4dBm.

The notation "dBu" is often found in the specifications in manuals that come with digital equipment. As was just mentioned, we know that the dBm is referenced to an impedance of 600 ohms. (This was derived from the early telephone company standards. Many of our audio standards originated with "Ma Bell.") However, most circuits today are bridging circuits instead of the older-style matching circuits, and the dBu is used as the unit of measure. Without going deeper into the subject of matching and bridging circuits, we can say that the dBu is equal to the dBm in most cases.

The Volume Unit

If the meters on the recording devices that we use to store digital audio displayed signal level in dBm, they would be very large and difficult to read. Considering the variety of system operating levels found on recording devices today, a comprehensive meter would have to range from −40dBm or −50dBm to +16dBm. This would be a range of around 76dB. To make this easier, we use the volume unit (VU) to measure signal level through the device. In most professional applications, this meter is calibrated so that an input level of +4dBm equals 0VU. However, if the device operates at −10dBm, as many consumer-type ones do, then −10dBm equals 0VU.

If a calibration tone of 1kHz at 0VU is played back from a consumer device operating at a level of −10dBm and from a professional device operating at +4dBm, the output level from the analog-to-digital converter will provide the same level to the storage medium in both cases. As this signal is played back from the storage medium, the converter outputs the calibration tone and produces a level of −10dBm or +4dBm at the device's output, depending on the device. The same signal played back on both devices will produce the reference level output at the device's specified line level. If we were to compare the output of the two devices, the +4dBm machine would play back 14dB louder, but this is due to the output gain of the playback section amplifier.

The classic VU meter is calibrated to conform to the impulse response of the human ear. The ear has an *impulse response,* or reaction time, that is defined as a response time and a decay time of about 300 milliseconds. This corresponds to the reaction time of the ear's stapedius muscle, which connects the three small bones of the middle ear to the eardrum. Therefore, any peak information shorter than 300 milliseconds will not be fully recognized by the meter. The

VU meter is designed to present the average content of the signal that passes through it.

The Peak Meter

On average, certain types of music have shorter attack and decay times than others, and, as you will see in chapter 2 during the discussions of digital recording, once full level is reached, there is no margin for error. A peak meter is a device that is designed to respond to all signals (no matter how short) that pass through it and is much more suitable for digital recording. The ballistics, or response time, of a standard DIN peak meter are designed to fulfill these requirements. A peak meter will reach full scale in 10 milliseconds. However, if the peak meter reaching the input signal were allowed to fall back at the same rate, the eye would be unable to follow its rapid movement. The metered value is held in a capacitor for a specified amount of time and allowed to fall back using a logarithmic response. Because the peak meter is not a volume indicator, it is correct to read it in decibels instead of volume units. Analog recording uses several standards for what is called the *zero level* for a peak meter. The International Electrotechnical Commission (IEC) has defined these meters as the BBC, where Mark 4 equals 0dBm; the Type 1, where 0dB equals +6dBm; and the Type 2, where 0dB equals 0dBm.

Traditionally, a volume indicator is calibrated so that there is some headroom above 0VU. Analog magnetic tape saturates slowly as levels rise, and typically 9dB of headroom above zero is allowed before reaching critical saturation levels. This scaling also accommodates peak information, as fast peaks tend to be about 9dB or 10dB higher than the average level. The BBC meters, as well as the Type 1 and Type 2 IEC meters, also allow for headroom above their zero reference. On the other hand, meters designed for digital audio are calibrated differently. Zero on a digital meter means full quantization level; that is, all bits at full value (there is no headroom). Therefore, it is important to note that 0VU on the console (whether it is +4dBm, −10dBm, or another level) does *not* equal 0dB on the digital meter. In many cases, −12dB was chosen as the calibration point for digital metering, but with the advent of systems with higher quantization levels, −18dB is sometimes used. To differentiate between peak meters and digital meters, the term "dBfs" is used ("fs" stands for "full scale"). This implies that the meter is on some kind of digital machine where 0dB equals full quantization level (all bits are used). However, manufacturers now use a variety of standards, and some allow several decibels of level above zero as a hidden headroom protection factor. Perhaps in the future a digital metering standard will be adapted that everyone can adhere to. In the meantime the prudent engineer will read the manual for the piece of equipment in use and be aware of its metering characteristics.

■ TIME CODE

Although not a basic characteristic or function of sound, *time code* is an important part of digital systems. Without time code, position locating and synchronization in the digital domain would be extremely difficult. Time code, as we know it today, was developed by the video industry to help with editing. In 1956, when videotape made its debut, the industry realized that the film process of cut-and-splice would not work in video. The images that were visible on film were not so on videotape. Certain techniques (e.g., magnetic ink that allowed you to see the recorded magnetic pulses) were developed, but these did not prove satisfactory. Another technique was to edit at the frame pulse or control track pulse located at the bottom edge of the videotape. This pulse tells the head how fast to switch in a rotating-head system. In the 1960s, electronic machine-to-machine editing was introduced, providing precise machine control and excellent frame-to-frame matchup. However, the splice point was still found by trial and error.

A system was needed that would uniquely number each frame so that it could be precisely located electronically. Several manufacturers introduced electronic codes to fulfill this task, but the codes were not compatible with one another. In 1969 the Society of Motion Picture and Television Engineers (SMPTE) developed a standard code that became recognized for its accuracy. That standard was also adopted by the European Broadcasting Union (EBU), making the code an international standard. The SMPTE/EBU code is the basis for all of today's professional video- and audiotape editing and synchronization systems.

The SMPTE time code is an addressable, reproducible, permanent code that stores location data in hours, minutes, seconds, and frames. The data consist of a binary pulse code that is recorded on the video- or audiotape along the corresponding video and audio signals. The advantages of this are (1) precise time reference, (2) interchange abilities among editing systems, and (3) synchronization between machines. The code can be stored in two different ways: longitudinal time code (LTC), which is stored on a separate audio track of the video or audio machine, and vertical interval time code (VITC), which is stored in the vertical blanking interval (i.e., between the fields and frames of the video picture). *Longitudinal time code,* used almost exclusively in audio-only applications, is an electronic signal that switches from one voltage to another, forming a string of pulses. Each 1-second-long piece of code is divided into 2,400 equal parts when used in the NTSC standard of 30 frames per second or into 2,000 equal parts when used with the PAL/SECAM system of 25 frames per second. Notice how each system generates a code word that is 80 bits long: PAL/SECAM: 2,000 bits per second divided by 25 frames per second equals 80 bits per frame; NTSC: 2,400 bits per second divided by 30 frames per second equals 80 bits per frame. Most of these bits have specific values that are counted only if the time code signal changes from one voltage to another in the middle of a bit period, forming a ½-bit pulse, which represents a digital 1, whereas a full-bit pulse represents a digital 0. Following is one frame's 80-bit code:

Bits	Function
0–3, 8, 9	Frame count
16–19, 24–26	Second count
32–35, 40–42	Minute count
48–51, 56, 57	Hour count
64–79	Sync word
10	Drop frame
11	Color frame
27	Field mark

The remaining eight groups of 4 bits are called *user bits,* which can be used to store data such as the date and reel number. Three bits are unused.

A typical time code number might be 18:23:45:28. This has a position 18 hours, 23 minutes, 45 seconds, and 28 frames into the event. This could be on the fortieth reel of tape. Time code does not need to start over on each reel.

Bit 10, the drop-frame bit, tells the time code reader whether the code was recorded in drop-frame or non-drop-frame format. Black-and-white television has a carrier frequency of 3.6MHz, whereas color uses 3.58MHz. This translates to 30 frames per second as opposed to 29.97 frames per second. To compensate for this, a defined number of frames are dropped from the time code every hour. The offset is 108 frames (3.6 seconds). Two frames are dropped every minute of every hour except in the tenth, twentieth, thirtieth, fortieth, and fiftieth minute. Frame dropping occurs at the changeover point from minute to minute.

Bit 11 is the color frame bit, which tells the system whether the color frame identification has been applied intentionally. Color frames are often locked as AB pairs to prevent color shift in the picture. As mentioned earlier, user bits can accommodate data for reel numbers, recording date, or any other information that can be encoded into eight groups of 4 bits.

Vertical interval time code is similar in format to LTC. It has a few more bits, and each of the 9 data-carrying bits is preceded by 2 sync bits. At the end of each frame there are eight *cyclic redundancy check* (CRC) codes, which are similar to the codes used in digital recording systems. This generates a total of 90 bits per frame. The main difference between LTC and VITC is how they are recorded on tape, LTC being recorded on one of the video tape's longitudinal audio tracks or on a spare track of the audiotape recorder. Some specialized two-track recorders have a dedicated time code track between the two standard audio tracks. Playback and record levels should be between −10dB and +3dB (−3dB is recommended). This allows 12dB of headroom on high-output audiotape operating at a reference level of 370 nanowebers per meter (nw/m), where +4dBm equals 370nw/m of magnetic fluxivity. Time code appears similar to a 400Hz square wave with many odd harmonics. Time code is difficult to read at low speeds and during fast wind or rewind.

Vertical interval time code was developed for use with 1-inch-tape-width helical scan SMPTE type-C video recorders, which are capable of slow-motion and freeze-frame techniques. During these functions LTC is impossible to read. However, VITC is readable (as long as the video is visible on the screen) because the indexing information for each field/frame is recorded in the video signal during the vertical blanking interval. Normally, VITC is recorded on two nonadjacent vertical blanking interval lines in both fields of each frame. Recording the code four times in each frame provides a redundancy error that lowers the probability of reading errors due to dropouts.

Because VITC is recorded as an integral part of the videotape recorder's video track, it can be read by the rotating video heads of a helical scan recorder at all times, even in freeze-frame or fast-wind modes. Video technology is explained more fully in chapter 4.

This ends our discussion of the basic characteristics of sound. An understanding of these concepts will help you with the information yet to come. We have touched only briefly on some very important areas, so you should consult the excellent general texts on sound and recording cited in the list of suggested readings at the end of this book.

TWO

The Digital Encoding Process

In chapter 1 we discussed the basic makeup of an analog signal, that is, a signal whose electrical form resembles the actual sound in the air. Simply stated, the electrical signal is analogous to the acoustic waveform. Earlier methods of storing sound relied on an analog process, where the electrical signal representing the acoustic sound is stored in a continuous, linear fashion. Systems such as the phonograph record, the Compact Cassette system, and analog magnetic reel-to-reel systems store the information as a series of either continuous physical or continuous magnetic representations of the sound. The grooves of a phonograph record modulate up, down, and sideways as the record spins, producing physical waveforms that can be retraced to retrieve the stored information. The patterns on magnetic tape are continuous areas of magnetic energy that vary in magnitude and spacing and that represent the original recorded waveform. These signals can be reproduced many times by dragging the magnetic pattern across a coil to produce an electrical signal that is sent to amplifiers and other devices in the playback chain.

The digital recording process, unlike the analog process, is discontinuous. Representing a continuous analog waveform with packets of digital information requires that we slice, or sample, the analog waveform into periodic pieces for storage. Sampling and quantization are the processes of looking at the incoming waveform periodically and defining the value or amplitude at each timed sample point.

■ SAMPLING

Sampling the waveform is the first task in the digitization process. How often does this need to be done? Four hundred times a second? Four thousand times a second? Four hundred thousand times a second? It turns out that an engineer named Henry Nyquist determined that if the sample rate is known, the frequency of a waveform can be defined by as few as two samples. Figure 2.1 shows a waveform that has been sampled twice. The sample rate is defined in terms of frequency, or the number of times per second the sample is taken. In our example the sample rate is 4Hz, or four times per second. Therefore, a sampling rate of 50kHz means that the waveform is being sampled 50,000 times per second. Note that there are two samples from the beginning of the waveform to where the waveform crosses the reference line in a positive direction. We know from our earlier discussion that a complete waveform starts at a reference pressure with an amplitude that moves in a positive direction (compression), followed by a rarefaction the creates a negative amplitude, and then, as the cycle completes, returns to the reference pressure. This completes one cycle. Figure 2.1 shows two sample periods, each ¼ second in length. Remember that *period* is the reciprocal of *frequency,*

Figure 2.1   Waveform sampling and the Nyquist frequency.

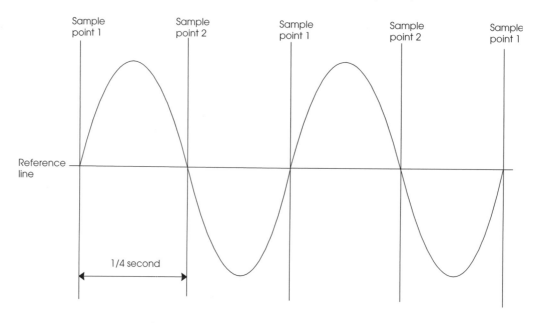

Sample point 1 Sample point 2 Sample point 1 Sample point 2 Sample point 1

Reference line

1/4 second

so a frequency of 4Hz has a period of ¼ second. The total period for the complete waveform in this example is ¼ second plus ¼ second, or ½ second. If the period is ½ second, the frequency of the waveform is 2Hz.

Let's take another example. Figure 2.2 shows a waveform sampled 32 times from the beginning of the wave to its end with a sample rate of, say, 40kHz:

$$\frac{32}{1} \times \frac{1}{40,000 \text{ s}} = \frac{32}{40,000 \text{ s}} = \frac{1}{2,500 \text{ s}}$$

Therefore, the wave has a frequency of 1,250Hz. Note that if we double the sample rate to 80kHz, the number of samples would double as well, and the answer to the problem would be the same.

Nyquist determined that because a minimum of two samples must be taken to determine the frequency of a waveform, the sample

Figure 2.2   Waveform sampling at a faster rate.

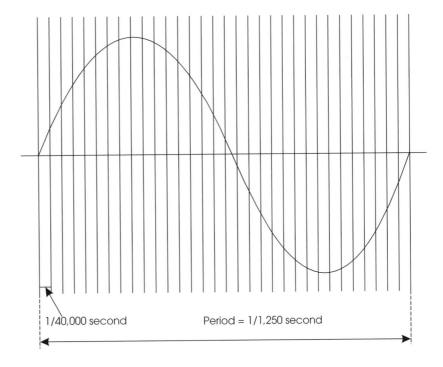

1/40,000 second   Period = 1/1,250 second

frequency must be at least twice the highest frequency that is to be recorded. Conversely, the highest desired frequency that can be accurately sampled must be slightly less than half the sample rate. This frequency is commonly referred to as the *Nyquist frequency.*

When a signal that is above the Nyquist frequency is sampled, *alias* (false) *frequencies* are created. That is, the system would define the time between the two samples as a frequency. These alias frequencies bear no harmonic relationship to the waveform that created them. In fact, the alias frequency folds down mathematically below the Nyquist point by the same amount it exceeded it. Aliasing is a distortion of the original signal, so it is important that alias frequencies be eliminated prior to digitizing the signal.

Aliasing is illustrated in figure 2.3. Note that although the wave has a frequency of 12kHz, it appears to be at a different frequency because we are sampling at 20kHz. In fact, because the Nyquist frequency for a sample rate of 20kHz is 10kHz, a 12kHz wave creates an alias frequency of 8kHz. Now the frequency of the waveform has been determined by sampling. The other piece of information we need is the amplitude of the signal, and this is accomplished through quantization.

Figure 2.3   Waveform sampling and aliasing.

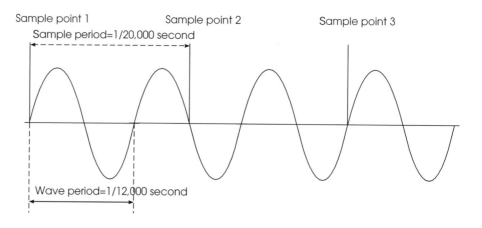

■ QUANTIZATION

Quantization is the process of determining the amplitude value of the waveform at each sample point and then encoding that value for storage. If we were to use a scale of amplitude from, for example, +1 volt to −1 volt for the maximum amplitude of the waveform, it would be easy to measure the amplitude of the waveform at each sample point. Figure 2.4 shows a waveform that has been sampled and the corresponding voltage at each sample point. It can be seen that sample point 1 is at .000 volts, point 2 at .625 volts, point 3 at 1.000 volts, point 4 at .625 volts, and point 5 back at .000 volts. Continuing with the wave's rarefaction (or negative) component, point 6 is at −.625 volts, point 7 at −1.000 volts, and point 8 at −.625 volts. The next point is the beginning of the next period. Storing these specific numbers in the magnetic domain is not possible because we can store magnetic pulses on a magnetic medium but cannot store, say, .625 volts.

Figure 2.4   Voltage assignments to a wave amplitude.

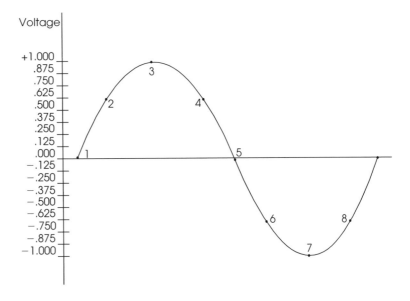

A number such as .625 uses a numbering system referred to as the *decimal system,* sometimes called the *base 10 system.* Different numbering systems are used in other engineering fields, including the hexadecimal (base 16), the octal (base 8), and the binary (base 2). Figure 2.5 compares these numbering systems.

Because it is easy to store pulses of different amplitudes on magnetic tape, a base 2 numbering system is ideal for codifying this data. We need to simply convert the decimal numbers into the binary system and then store the number as a series of pulses on the magnetic medium. In chapters 4 and 5, we look at the various types of storage media, some of which may not be magnetic, but for now, we assume a storage system based on magnetic tape.

Two of the more popular ways of encoding this information are the two's complement method and the offset binary method. In the two's complement method, two ascending binary counts are used with the first bit representing the sign of the value. The offset binary method uses the absolute binary value of the voltage, with the first bit once again representing the sign. Figure 2.6, using the voltages from our previous example in figure 2.4, shows these two methods.

The Dynamic Range of a Digital System

Another important factor in the quantization process of an analog waveform is the resolution of the coding system. Each digit in the binary system is called a *bit.* Each group of bits is called a *word.* Therefore, a group, such as that representing $-.875$ volts in figure 2.6, is called a 4-bit word. The greater the number of bits in the word, the higher the resolution of that word. For example, a 2-bit word gives the possibility of 2^2, or 4, data values, where the integer is the number of possible states (1 or 0) and the exponent the number of bits in the word. Using our example of ± 1 volt for the total amplitude of the waveform allows us to assign a value of 0 volts, .25 volts, .5 volts, or 1 volt to the positive part of the waveform and the same amount (using the offset binary method or two's complement method) for the negative part. This resolution is not suitable for a complex audio waveform. However, note that the number of possibilities expands exponentially as the number of bits in the word increases. A 4-bit word gives 2^4, or 16, possible values for both the positive and the negative parts of the waveform, whereas an 8-bit word gives 2^8, or 256, possible values.

Knowing the number of bits in the data stream at each sample point allows the amplitude potential of the digital signal to be determined. Because each added bit doubles the number of usable values,

Figure 2.5 Comparison of quantization numbering systems.

Decimal (base 10)	Octal (base 8)	Hexadecimal (base 16)	Binary (base 2)
0	0	0	0
1	1	1	1
2	2	2	10
3	3	3	11
4	4	4	100
5	5	5	101
6	6	6	110
7	7	7	111
8	10	8	1000
9	11	9	1001
10	12	A	1010
11	13	B	1011
12	14	C	1100
13	15	D	1101
14	16	E	1110
15	17	F	1111
16	20	10	10000
17	21	11	10001
18	22	12	11010

the voltage potential of the signal is effectively doubled; therefore, the 20(1ogX) formula applies. Chapter 1 showed that 20(1og2) = 6dB. Therefore, each bit represents about 6dB of dynamic range (signal-to-noise ratio). The greater the number of bits in the signal, the larger the possible dynamic range. This is a simplistic representation of the dynamic range of a digital system as we are really describing the signal-to-error ratio, for which some advanced mathematics are required. For now we can say that the dynamic range of a digital signal can be determined by multiplying the number of bits by 6.

How much dynamic range is needed to record music? Figure 1.6 in chapter 1 showed decibel levels for various sounds relative to the threshold of hearing. Note that the level for a full symphony orchestra was about 90dB and that for a chamber orchestra about 70dB. A typical amplified rock band can easily approach levels of 120dB. However, because residual background noise covers very soft sounds (because of the masking effect), a full 120dB of dynamic capability is not required. In fact, a sound source with 120dB of dynamic range that is used to reproduce the acoustic levels for the loud parts would need to be above the threshold of pain for us to

Figure 2.6 Offset binary and two's complement methods.

Voltage Readings	Offset Binary Method	Two's Complement Method
+1.000	10000	00001
.875	1111	0111
.750	1110	0110
.625	1101	0101
.500	1100	0100
.375	1011	0011
.250	1010	0010
.125	1001	0001
.000	1000	0000
−.125	0111	1111
−.250	0110	1110
−.375	0101	1101
−.500	0100	1100
−.625	0011	1011
−.750	0010	1010
−.875	0001	1001
−1.000	0000	1000

hear the soft parts in an average environment. The best analog storage media, such as magnetic tape at 15 inches per second in the half-track format, have a total dynamic range of about 84dB from the noise floor to the 3 percent distortion point. The average phonograph record (remember those?) has a range of about 65dB, whereas FM radio has a range of about 70dB. Early digital systems used 14-bits per word and had a dynamic range of about 84dB to 86dB, which proved to be too limiting, so later systems used 16 bits per word. In fact, this became the standard word length for the Compact Disc, which has a dynamic range of 96dB or better. Today, some feel that this resolution is not sufficient, and some 20- and even 24-bit systems are commonly used. However, the current standard for consumer audio is 16 bits, and because the final product is for use in the consumer world, 20- and 24-bit professional audio master recordings must be processed down to 16 bits for the Compact Disc.

Quantization Error   Because a discrete number of steps are available during the quantization of the waveform (because of the number of bits in the system) and because the analog signal is continuous, there will always be a value at some sample point that falls between any two steps. When this occurs, the system must decide whether to round up or down to the nearest available step. In the worst case, the value will be exactly between the two quantization levels and may toggle back and forth, causing an undesirable noise. Therefore, the maximum amount of quantization error in a digital system equals $\pm \frac{1}{2}$ the quantization interval. This error is heard as a kind of white noise or graininess, not unlike tape hiss at various amplitude signals. At high levels the error will likely be masked by the signal itself, but as the level drops and the error correlates to the signal, the error begins to sound like distortion. The error becomes bothersome because of the correlation factor.

Dither   An analog noise signal is often added to the waveform that is to be digitized to combat the effects of quantization error on low-level signals. This signal, called *dither,* not only helps mask the quantization error but also helps force the toggling bits to be rounded up to the nearest level, thus effectively lowering the quantization error of the complex signal. The error then correlates with the noise and not with the signal being recorded. Because the noise is constant, the quantization error stays constant and does not change with the recorded signal. Another way to lower quantization noise is to raise the number of bits in the digital word. Each additional bit lowers the correlated error by 6dB.

Digital Modulation Systems   A modulation system is simply a way to encode the digital signal on a storage medium. A way is needed to represent the 1s and 0s of the binary code. The output of the analog-to-digital converter is a series of pulses whose amplitude varies with the amplitude of the original waveform. This series or string of pulses is called *pulse amplitude modulation* (PAM). As these pulses are measured and quantized to binary numbers (a code), the signal becomes a *pulse code modulation* (PCM) signal. The most popular system today is the PCM method, although other systems are used, such as *pulse position modulation* (PPM) and *pulse width modulation* (PWM). Figure 2.7 shows several of these systems. Pulse width modulation is often referred to as pulse density modulation (PDM).

Figure 2.7   A waveform and different types of digital encoding.

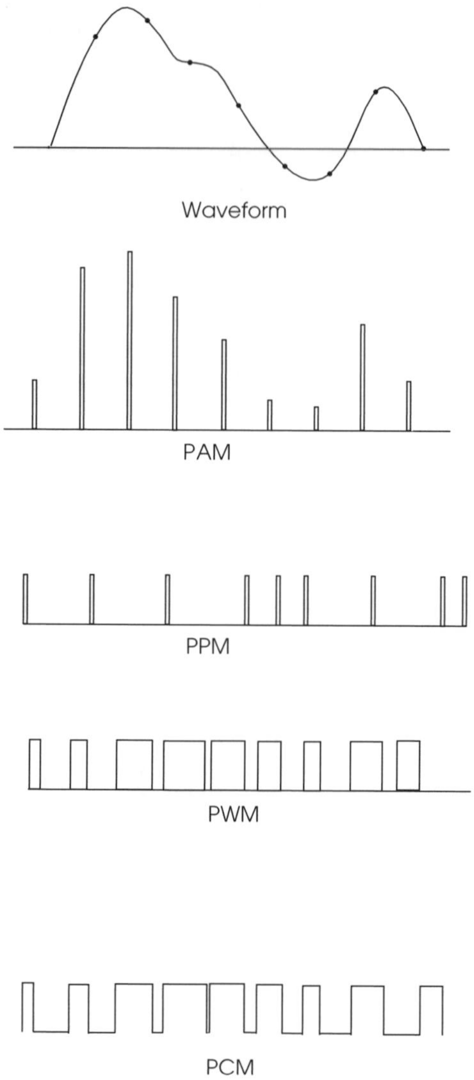

Waveform

PAM

PPM

PWM

PCM

■ ANALOG-TO-DIGITAL CONVERSION

Now that we have discussed and seen the principles of sampling and quantization, let's look in more detail at what occurs when a signal passes through the entire analog-to-digital conversion process.

We call the whole device an analog-to-digital converter, but several steps occur in the analog domain prior to digitization. Figure 2.8 shows a block diagram of a typical PCM analog-to-digital converter. Let's discuss this diagram step by step.

Input Amplifier (a.)

As a signal enters the analog-to-digital converter, it is amplified to a level appropriate to the design of the converter. This level varies, depending on the converter manufacturer and on whether the signal that is set to the converter originates from a −10dBm or a +4dBm source. All converters are designed for use with line-level sources. Microphones must be sent through a suitable preamplifier to raise their signal strength to line level prior to digitization.

Dither Generator (b.)

As discussed previously, the digitizing process inevitably contains some amount of quantizing error that is equal to half the distance between the smallest quantization steps. Recall that dither is low-

Figure 2.8 Block diagram of a PCM analog-to-digital converter.

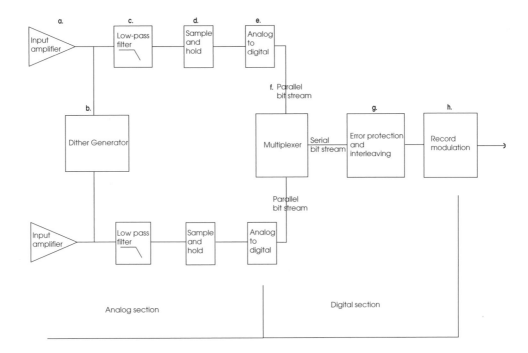

level, random (Gaussian) noise that is added to the signal being digitized. The amount of dither used is typically about one-third the value of the *least significant bit* (⅓ LSB). The LSB is the last bit in the digital word, and the value ⅓ LSB represents about 2dB. Increasing the broad-band noise of the system reduces the correlated distortion that is caused by the digitizing process.

Anti-Aliasing Filter (c.)

In our discussion of sampling we saw that aliasing occurs if frequencies above half the sample rate are allowed to enter the system. A filter prevents this from occurring. Note that the dither generator is implemented prior to the anti-aliasing filter because the dither signal might contain frequencies above the Nyquist frequency. This filter, to be effective, must have a steep cutoff characteristic. Although filter design is beyond the scope of this book, a brief discussion of filter types might be helpful.

Typically, an analog filter consists of a series of reactive components that might include an inductor and a capacitor. Every filter has a turnover frequency and a slope. The turnover frequency is determined by the formula

$$F = \frac{1}{2\pi\tau}$$

where F is the turnover frequency, π is pi (about 3.14), and τ is tau (time) in microseconds. Every reactive component has a time constant, or the amount of time a signal is delayed after passing through this reactive component, whether an inductor or a capacitor. In the above formula tau is the total delay time for all components in the network. For example, if the time constant total in the circuit is 50 microseconds, the frequency where the filter begins its downward slope is 3,150Hz.

The slope of the filter is determined by the order of the filter. Simply put, the slope is the number of single-filter sets that are cascaded together. Each filter order generates a downward slope at the turnover frequency of 6dB per octave. A second-order filter slopes at 12dB per octave, a third-order filter slopes at 18dB per octave, and so on. Figure 2.9 shows a typical filter. The frequencies prior to the slope constitute the *pass band* and those after the slope the *stop band.* Higher-order filters also increase the depth of the *attenuation* (reduction in level) provided by the filter.

The anti-aliasing filter must have a very steep slope and very high attenuation to be effective. The amount of attenuation should equal

Figure 2.9   Filter schematics.

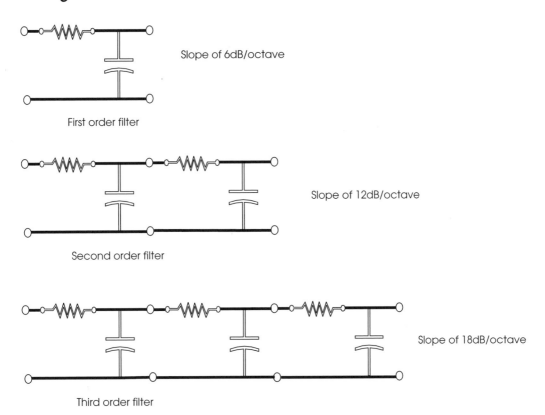

Slope of 6dB/octave

First order filter

Slope of 12dB/octave

Second order filter

Slope of 18dB/octave

Third order filter

the dynamic range of the digital system. In the case of a 16-bit word, the amount of attenuation should be about 96dB or greater. Ideally, the slope should be ∞ (infinity) dB per octave, or effectively no slope at all, but simply a straight cutoff. This is shown in figure 2.10a, where the pass band is 1kHz to 20kHz, the turnover frequency 20kHz, and the stop band 20kHz and higher. However, analog filter designs have a couple of problems in this area. First, it is impossible to construct an analog filter with a "brick-wall" slope. Second, whenever a signal passes through a reactive component, the component's time constant causes the signal above the turnover frequency to be delayed, causing the signal below the turnover frequency to arrive at the output of the device before the portion of the signal above the turnover frequency. This creates a problem called group delay, which results in phase anomalies in the pass band signal. Other artifacts of very steep analog filters are *ringing* and *overshoot*.

Figure 2.10 Various filter slopes for anti-aliasing.

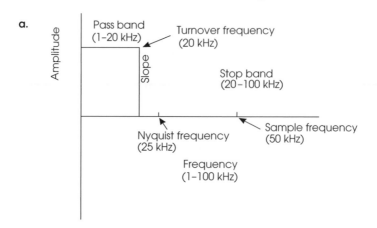

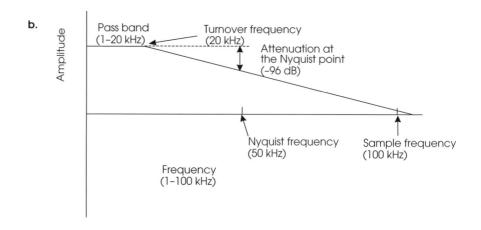

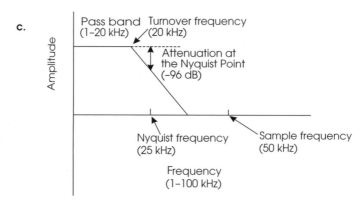

One solution to the filter problem is to increase the sample rate sufficiently to move the Nyquist point far enough above the turnover frequency so that a gentle slope can be used while providing the proper amount of attenuation. This is shown in figure 2.10b. However, this greatly increases the amount of storage space required for the digital signal because storage is a function of sample rate and word length. The most frequently used sample rates are 44.1kHz and 48kHz. Later we will see why these frequencies were chosen.

In the analog domain the best solution is to tailor the slope of the filter for the proper amount of attenuation at the Nyquist point and simply accept the phase and frequency anomalies that occur. Limiting the slope to the minimum required rate and adjusting the turnover point to as low a frequency as possible keeps these anomalies caused by filtering to a minimum. This is shown in figure 2.10c. However, in practice the turnover frequency is about 20kHz. This frequency was chosen because it was thought to be above the range of human hearing.

Later in this chapter, we will see that after the signal is in the digital domain, brick-wall filtering can be implemented easily. You will see how this is accomplished in the discussion of oversampling converters.

Sample and Hold (d).

The next section of the analog-to-digital converter in figure 2.8 is the sample-and-hold circuit. Here the audio wave is sampled at a periodic rate and the value of the sample held until the next sample period. This circuit does a very important job because any variation in the value of the data prior to the next sample period results in inaccurate data. The sample-and-hold circuit maintains the value of the sample until the next circuit in the chain (the analog-to-digital circuit) can quantize the value and output a binary word. If the value were to vary prior to quantization, the amplitude value of the waveform at that point would be incorrect. In essence, this circuit consists of a clock-driven switch and a capacitor that holds the sample value until the next clock tick. Figure 2.11 shows a waveform and the steps that occur as the wave is sampled. Figure 2.11a of the figure shows the wave and the sample points, figure 2.11b the value, or amplitude, of each sample, and figure 2.11c how the value of each sample is held until the next sample point. Part d shows the original wave superimposed on the sample-and-hold values.

In the digital signal a type of distortion called *jitter* is produced if the clock is not extremely accurate. Jitter manifests itself as modulation noise on playback. If the clock pulse does not line up with the

Figure 2.11   The sample-and-hold process.

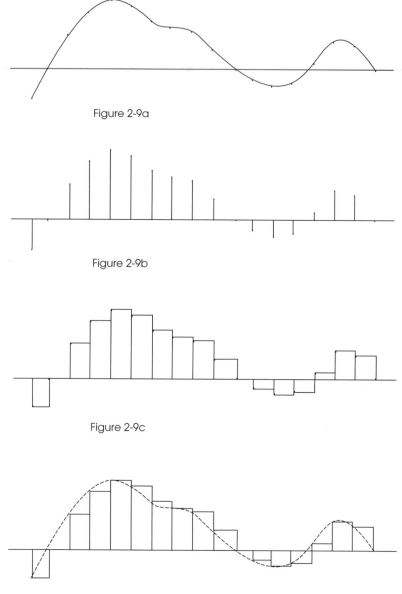

Figure 2-9a

Figure 2-9b

Figure 2-9c

Figure 2-9d

beginning of the digital word, jitter may cause the sampled value to differ from the actual value at the sample point. Jitter is especially evident in high-amplitude, high-frequency signals. Because fewer samples per waveform occur as the frequency increases, the errors per waveform increase as well.

Analog-to-Digital Conversion (e.)

Sample-and-hold values are converted to binary words at this point. Typically, the held value is allowed to decrease to zero, and the time this takes is used to generate the binary word. Another approach compares the value of the current sample against a reference value to output a digital word that is proportional to the known value. Speed and accuracy are of the utmost importance. A new value is required at every sample period, and this value must be accurately timed against the evenly spaced steps of the sample clock. In a 16-bit quantization system sampled at 44.1kHz, the converter outputs a word to a resolution of 65,536 (2^{16}) steps, 44,100 times per second, or once every 22.67 microseconds! In this case, 16 1s or 0s are output simultaneously as a parallel word from the 16 outputs of the analog-to-digital converter.

Multiplexing (f.)

Today, parallel word storage is very difficult and expensive and is best accomplished on RAM (random access memory) or ROM (read-only memory) chips. This might be fine for some samplers that need to store only short pieces of data, but it is not practical for works such as Beethoven's Ninth Symphony, which is about 71 minutes long. Imagine trying to store parallel data for that on magnetic tape. You would need 16 parallel tracks for one channel of audio information or 32 tracks for stereo—not a very practical way to record and store data. Modern digital multitracks of 24 or 48 channels store one channel of information on each track, so storing 24 16-bit channels in a parallel form would require 384 tracks.

Analog and digital recorders can be thought of as serial devices; that is, the data are stored linearly along the tape. Each recorded channel requires a single linear (serial) data stream. As we will see, several channels may be combined in a single stream for storage. However, the first step is to convert the 16-bit parallel word to a serial bit stream. This is accomplished in the multiplexer section of the analog-to-digital converter, where the parallel data are output as a serial bit stream using shift registers. Each bit is output sequentially (on the basis of the sample rate) to the next stage of the digitizing process. Figure 2.12 shows a shift register device. The clock rate tells each register when to output its bit into the serial stream.

Figure 2.12   A multiplexer block schematic.

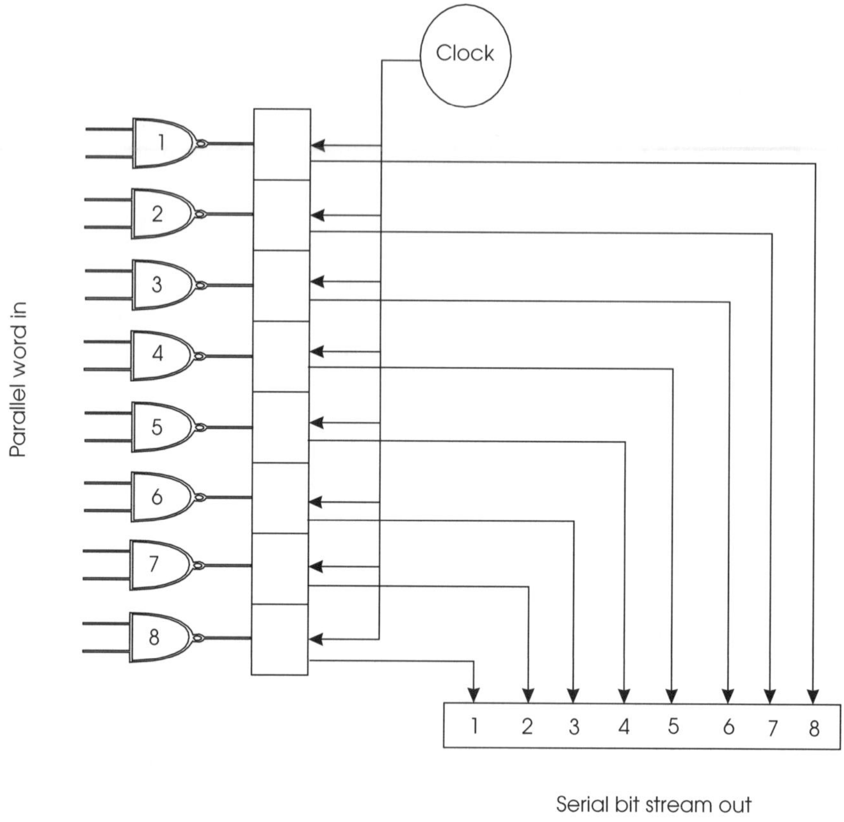

■ **Added Bits**   Some additional bits are added to the stream in the multiplexer. These bits, sometimes referred to as *preambles* or *synchronization bits,* identify the beginning of each word in the serial stream, which usually consists of a series of 4 bits that would not naturally occur in any other situation. These 4 bits are sometimes referred to as *frame identifiers.* Bits can also be added to identify the sample frequency, to provide data locations, to signify preemphasis of the signal, and even to define SMPTE time code.

Error Protection and Interleaving (g.)   Dropouts, an unfortunate feature of magnetic media, are caused by several things. Debris on the tape itself can cause the tape to lift away momentarily from the playback head, or a void on the tape can result from an inaccurate coating of the magnetic oxide. Another culprit is dirt in the tape path. Poor calendaring (smoothing) may cause the surface of the tape to be uneven. Magnetic and magneto-optical disks are subject to these problems as well. On optical media, such as the compact disc and the pre-recorded mini-disc, information losses may be caused by scratches and dirt as well as by vibration and mistracking.

Dropouts occurring on analog magnetic tape often are not noticeable. If the machine is moving tape at a speed of 15 inches per second or greater, the dropout must be very large before it becomes audible. If the sound at that point is complex and loud, the masking effect may cover the dropout. Additionally, analog noise reduction systems help mask dropouts. However, dropouts in the digital domain mean something very different in that they may cause many digital words to be missed during the reproduce stage of the digital-to-analog converter. Large dropouts (called *burst errors* in digital audio) may result in the absence of enough digital data to prevent the decoder from reconstructing the original waveform. Several processes occur to make the digital bit stream as robust as possible and to allow the system to correct errors caused by the storage medium (see point G in figure 2.6).

First, parity bits and CRC codes are added to the bit stream. These data are derived from the original serial bit stream and therefore are redundant. Parity bits and CRC codes help to detect and correct errors. Second, the bit stream undergoes *interleaving,* which mixes up (reorders) the digital 1s and 0s and places them at alternate locations within the bit stream. As long as the formula or code for interleaving is known, the reverse can happen prior to decoding to restore the data to their original order. Figure 2.13 shows an example of simple interleaving. The original data stream (numbers 1–15) was first interleaved or reordered simply by taking every other number. The second interleave then applied the same process to the first. Note here that although a burst error has taken out four consecutive data packets in the twice-interleaved data stream, de-interleaving causes no consecutive data losses in the digital stream. This does not indicate or correct the errors, but it does make it easier to interpolate the missing data because the error is not within neighboring data packets. Different digital formats make use of their own interleaving codes.

Because errors occur, a system was developed to detect the difference between good data and incorrect data. The CRC code is used as an efficient error detection system. Packets of digital information, called *blocks,* are examined at fixed, regular intervals. Each data block is divided by a fixed, arbitrarily selected number; the

Figure 2.13   Interleaving.

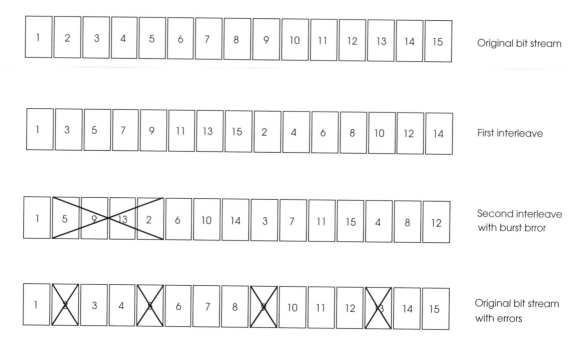

quotient ignored; and the binary remainder added to the end of the block. This is the CRC code for this data block. On playback the same data block is divided by the same arbitrary number, the quotient discarded, and the remainder (most often called a *block code*) compared to the block's CRC code. A difference indicates an error in that block. However, additional data are needed to repair the errors.

A parity block is also created from the digital block. This block, called the *parity code,* is also added to the serial bit stream. An example of a parity code using three simple 5-bit blocks of data follows:

Data block 1	10111
Data block 2	10101
Data block 3	01100
Parity block	01110

The three binary data blocks are added together and the carried values discarded. Therefore, binary $1 + 1 + 0 = 0$ when the carried 1 is discarded. On playback, this parity word is used to help further detect and then correct any error that is found. The serial bit stream's processing order is actually the reverse of what we have discussed. All the additional bits, including CRC and parity data, are added to the stream prior to interleaving. After interleaving the serial bit stream is sent to the record modulation circuit.

Record Modulation (h.)

The binary serial data stream is converted to a form usable by the storage medium at this point. The data's density—which has been steadily increasing with the changes from parallel to serial, the additional preambles, the CRCs, and parity bits—is now reduced, by coding, into a data stream for storage. This must occur whether the storage is on magnetic tape or another media. There are as many codes available as there are formats. For example, stationary-head systems use either the HDM-1 code (Sony's high-density modulation system) or the 4/6M (4-to-6 modulation) code. The Digital Audio Tape (DAT) recorder uses an 8/10 group code, and the Compact Disc uses an EFM (8-to-14 modulation) code. All these are often called *channel codes.* The code is then sent to the recording mechanism, where, in the case of magnetic tape, the positive impulses (1s) and the negative impulses (0s) are converted to near-positive and near-negative saturations, respectively, on the medium. No bias is required because we do not care about the linearity of the magnetic recording itself as long as the 1s and 0s are represented accurately. In the case of optical and magneto-optical media, the data are represented by pits or nonpits and north or south magnetic polarities.

You may also find the preemphasis circuit here. Many early digital recording systems were plagued with broad-band noise. Because such noise is characterized by rising frequency response and equal energy per frequency (i.e., white noise), it is more apparent in the higher frequencies. An early attempt at noise reduction in the analog domain used a passive complementary system that raised the high frequencies prior to recording and then lowered them by the same amount on playback. This technique, applied by some early digital systems as well, was applied to the signal after digitization but prior to record modulation. This preemphasis used time constants of 50 microseconds (the same as in some analog tape systems) and 15 microseconds and was constructed as a single-order filter with a slope of 6dB per octave between the frequencies of 3.183kHz and 10.611kHz, respectively. Complementary postequalization was then applied at the playback demodulation stage. A bit in the digital bit stream was toggled between a 1 and a 0 to tell the digital-to-analog converter whether emphasis was applied during recording.

You can see that the analog-to-digital conversion process is complicated and that any errors in the process may result in an inaccurately generated binary pulse code. In the next chapter we examine the digital-to-analog process to see how the PCM bit stream can be successfully converted back to the original analog waveform. In chapters 4 and 5, we examine the storage mediums themselves.

THREE

The Digital Decoding Process

We have now converted the analog waveform into a digital signal that is suitable for long-term storage and retrieval. Chapters 4 and 5 address the formats available for storing the digital data, but for now let's examine how the data are reconstructed after retrieval from whatever storage medium we want to use. Figure 3.1 shows a block diagram of the digital-to-analog conversion process.

■ PLAYBACK DEMODULATION (a.)

The first step in the process of recovering the original waveform is playback demodulation. Initially, the data were applied to the record head from the record modulation circuit as a square-wave type of signal. However, during the recording-and-storage process, some high-frequency information in the square wave may have been lost. Remember that we do not really care about the linearity of the storage medium, so some high-frequency loss in the data stream (but not in the actual audio information) is acceptable. Recall from chapter 1 that a square wave is actually a sine wave with added odd harmonics, some of which are lost in the storage-and-recovery process. A wave reshaper circuit restores the sharp transitions of the positive or negative pulse changes and effectively restores the square-wave characteristics of the signal. Figure 3.2 shows how the data may look after recovery and after reshaping.

Figure 3.1   Block diagram of a digital-to-analog converter.

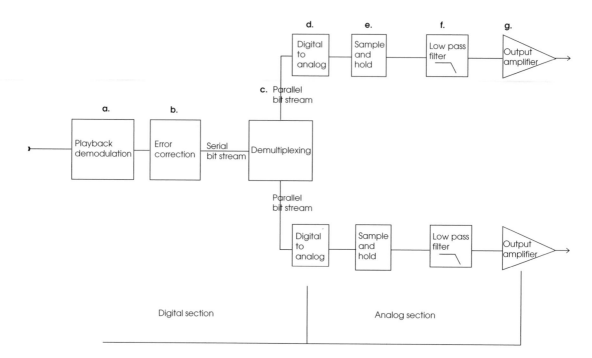

Next, the opposite of the modulation scheme used in the record-ing process is applied. Whether it is HDM-1, EFM, or 4/6M, or another code, these data are usually converted to a simple non-return-to-zero (NRZ) code, which simply defines a binary 1 for high-amplitude states and a binary 0 for low-amplitude states. The recov-ered, reshaped, demodulated bit stream is then sent to the next stage in the process.

■ ERROR DETECTION AND CORRECTION (b.)

After the bit stream is demodulated, it is de-interleaved using a reversal of the original interleaving scheme. Recall from figure 2.11 in chapter 2 that errors that occurred in the storage medium are minimized by the de-interleaving process. Any burst errors will have

Figure 3.2 Reshaping the bit stream.

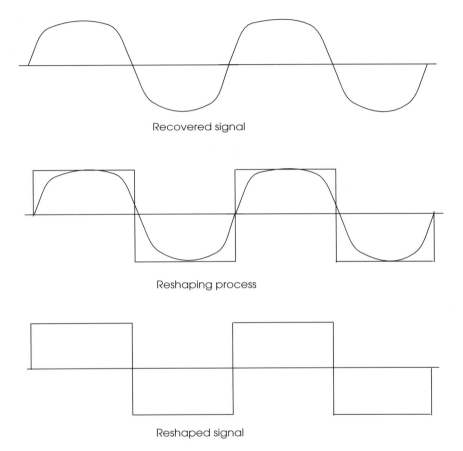

Recovered signal

Reshaping process

Reshaped signal

the incorrect data spread out so that no consecutive errors are included in the bit stream. This is not to say that consecutive errors never occur after de-interleaving; rather, such errors are rare. The data are now put into a buffer, where they are clocked out at the rate they were sampled at. Synchronization bits are used to align the bits to the sample rate. This buffer stage is important because it reduces the amount of timing errors, or jitter problems, to nearly zero.

The CRC code is then examined and compared to the data blocks to detect any errors in the digital word. If an error is detected, the parity word comes into play. Recall from chapter 2 that a block parity code was created from the original data. Now suppose that the CRC code has determined that an error in data block 2 exists:

Original data

Data block 1	10111
Data block 2	10101
Data block 3	01100
Parity block	01110

Recovered data

Data block 1	10111	
Data block 2	01011	(incorrect)
Data block 3	01100	
Parity block	01110	

The three data blocks are now summed with the original parity block to form a new parity block: 11110. Then the new parity block is summed with the incorrect word. This binary addition generates a new, corrected data block:

New parity block	11110
Data block 2	01011 (incorrect)
New data block 2	10101 (correct)

The corrected block is now inserted back into the bit stream, restoring the stream of data to its originally recorded values.

However, what if the CRC code was incorrect and the data word was correct? The CRC code would then identify a block as incorrect even thought it is not. As seen below, when the new parity block is summed with the block thought to be incorrect, the corrected word is the same as the original block if there really is no error:

Recovered data

Data block 1	10111
Data block 2	10101 (noted as incorrect)
Data block 3	01100
Original parity block	01110
New parity block	00000 (sum of data and parity blocks)
Corrected data block 2	10101 (same as original)

Systems may also use error identification and correction schemes where more than one parity block is generated per word. These so-called Hamming Code systems generate parity information for each section of the 16-bit (or greater) digital word effectively performing error correction several times on each word.

Now, let's suppose that an error is detected but cannot be corrected by the existing parity information. A burst error may well have obliterated the digital audio information as well as the CRC code and parity information. The system would detect an error from this massive loss of data but not have the data available for correction. In many systems data are recorded redundantly; that is, identical data are recorded in several locations on the medium at once. In this case, the decoder's first response will be to find the alternate

data location from the address code in the preamble. If this is not possible, other methods of correction must be used.

If redundancy fails or is not available on a system, the second method of error correction is called linear interpolation. Audio is a continuous signal in that one portion of a wave logically follows another. Therefore, if the stream of data were proceeding sequentially (e.g., from 1 to 10) and the number 8 were missing, it would be easy to determine the missing number. A string of voltages—for example, .1, .2, .3, .4, .5, .6, .7, blank, .9—can be repaired by simply taking the value preceding the blank, summing it with the value after the blank, and dividing by 2 (the average). The result is .8 volts. To correct errors of this type when no parity information is available, the digital system derives missing data that should logically fit between two known values (see figure 3.3).

A third method of error correction is used when, even after de-interleaving, successive errors in the bit stream cannot be corrected by the first two methods. Here the system simply repeats the preceding value, or holds the existing one. This is often called *lateral interpolation* or *word value holding.* A combination of linear and lateral interpolation may be used, depending on the quantity of successive errors.

Finally, when all else fails and the error cannot be corrected or substituted for by the previous three methods, the decoder simply mutes the output during the interval of time taken up by the noncorrectable error. The data word in question is changed to all zeroes, and the decoder mutes the output. The three methods are shown in Figure 3.3. It takes a great number of successive muted errors before this becomes noticeable. The integration time of the human ear is said to be between 20 and 30 milliseconds. At a sample rate of 48kHz, it would take about 1,000 successive muted digital errors before we would perceive a gap in the music; and if the music is very complex, it may not be noticeable even then. A click, overload distortion, or flutter (a type of distortion) in analog tape is relatively audible, and although we might experience a brief roughness or edge to the sound, an absence of sound is much less noticeable.

■ DEMULTIPLEXING (c.)

After the serial bit stream has been de-interleaved and the error correction system has found, corrected, or concealed the storage-induced errors, the data need to be demultiplexed. Recall from

Figure 3.3   Three error correction possibilities.

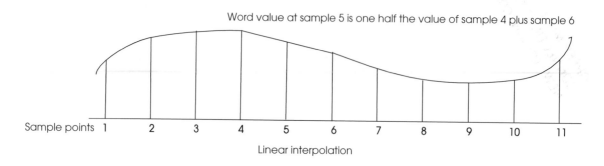

Word value at sample 5 is one half the value of sample 4 plus sample 6

Sample points 1   2   3   4   5   6   7   8   9   10   11

Linear interpolation

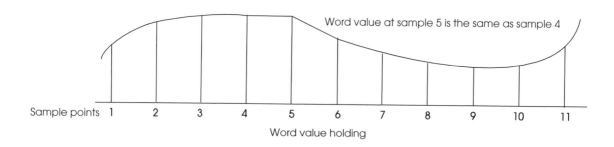

Word value at sample 5 is the same as sample 4

Sample points 1   2   3   4   5   6   7   8   9   10   11

Word value holding

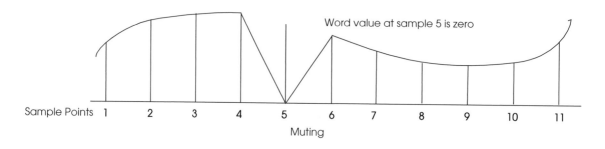

Word value at sample 5 is zero

Sample Points 1   2   3   4   5   6   7   8   9   10   11

Muting

chapter 2 that the analog-to-digital converter output a parallel word that was then converted to a serial bit stream. For the data to be converted back into recognizable analog levels, the reverse occurs. The serial data are loaded sequentially into a parallel output shift register device that holds all data bits until the complete word is received. The preamble (address bits) signifies the beginning of each new word to the multiplexer, which then outputs the parallel word to the digital-to-analog converter for further processing.

■ DIGITAL-TO-ANALOG CONVERTER (d.)

Here the 16-bit (or greater) digital words are converted back into analog voltage levels. The clock-driven demultiplexer delivers a parallel word to the analog-to-digital converter, which then generates an analog voltage that is based on the same scaling as the converter. This can be done by the two's complement method or the offset binary method, depending on the encoder, to define the positive and negative amplitude values. The two main strategies for this process are the weighted resistor network and the dual slope–integrating converter. The *weighted resistor network* has a switch for each bit and a corresponding resistor that represents the value of each bit. A reference voltage is applied to the resistors where a binary 1 closes the switch and allows current to flow and a binary 0 holds the switch in the open position preventing the current flow from that part of the resistor network. The greater the resistance in each branch, the less voltage is allowed to pass. The resistors are valued so that the most significant bit (MSB) passes through the least resistance, with the value of the resistors increasing exponentially until the least significant bit (LSB). Figure 3.4 shows a typical 8-bit weighted resistor network. If the resistance is equal to r, then the MSB resistor will be $2r$, the next 2^2r, and so on until the last resistor, which for the LSB will be 2^8r. This is 256 times the value of the first resistor. Note that this corresponds to the number of bits in the system and the quantizing steps available. An 8-bit system would have 2^8 (256) quantizing steps. The output of all the resistors (one for each bit) are summed, and a corresponding voltage is generated. The 8-bit word that is generating the current flow would be 11101011, as seen by the switch settings in the figure.

The *dual slope-integrating converter* (see figure 3.5) uses a counter to induce a delay, after which a discharge pulse is generated. The value of the delay is based on the value of the digital input word. The field effect transistor (FET) controls the charging of the capacitor. The final charge across the capacitor is the analog value of the digital word. The control logic circuit then issues the discharge command, and the analog voltage is output. The word is divided into two sections, and in this case the 16-bit word is divided into upper and lower counters, each handling 8 bits. New methods of analog-to-digital conversion are constantly being developed, and the two examples cited here are by no means used in all systems. However, they are typical of the types of devices used to generate the analog voltages necessary for conversion of the PCM digital signal back to a clone of the original analog waveform.

Figure 3.4 An 8-bit weighted resistor network converter.

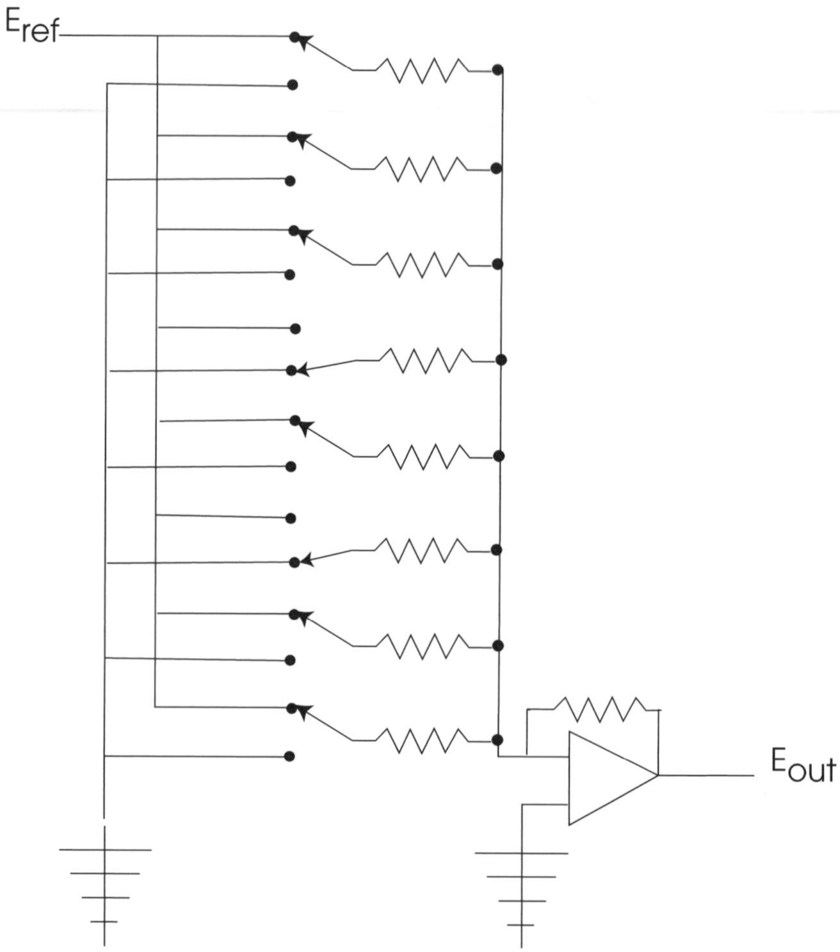

■ SAMPLE AND HOLD (e.)

An additional network, the sample-and-hold network, is needed to recover the original analog waveform. The digital-to-analog converter's output voltages are in a pulse form that represents the amplitudes of the signal at the sample point. The duration of these

Figure 3.5   A dual slope-integrating converter.

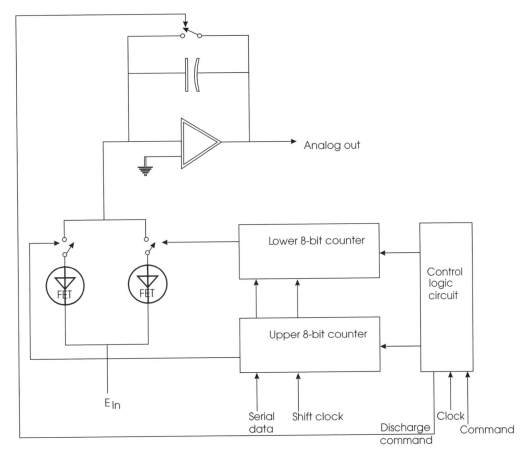

pulses varies, depending on the type of converter used. Ideally, the output of the converter is a series of pulses, each occupying the space of the original sample, but this is never the case. The space, or lack thereof, between the pulses is often referred to as an aperture, the size of which is directly proportional to the frequency response of the system. High frequencies can be attenuated by as much as 4dB if the pulse is held until the next sample point. However, if the pulse's hold time is too short, the signal-to-noise ratio of the system is reduced.

As is often experienced in audio engineering, a gain on one hand is often offset by a loss on the other. Therefore, although infinitely short pulses allow flat frequency response, fully held pulses provide the lowest noise floor. Because the noise of the system is also defined by the number of bits used, the best solution is to find a hold time that does not compromise the signal-to-quantization ratio but that does provide the minimum high-frequency roll-off. A maximum hold time of $\frac{1}{4}$ of the sample period seems to be the best compromise, as the high-frequency loss is less than $\frac{1}{3}$ dB at 20kHz and the system's signal-to-noise ratio is not compromised. Figure 3.6 shows these conditions.

■ RECONSTRUCTION FILTER (f.)

The output low-pass filter, sometimes called the reconstruction filter, is the final section in the process of transforming the stored digital signal back to its original analog format. The waveform output by the sample-and-hold circuit is a staircase waveform, as shown in figure 3.7a. This waveform contains many odd harmonics that are a function of the square-wave-like signal. A filter (similar to the input anti-aliasing filter) is used to remove these harmonics and recover the smooth, continuous nature of the original wave.

Another way to view this is to consider the staircase waveform as a pulse amplitude–modulated signal. Looking at the spectrum of the sample pulses, we see that side-band images of that spectrum appear above and below the sample frequency. The original audio signal is included in the base band, so the frequencies that are contained above $\frac{1}{2}$ the sample frequency need to be filtered out. The filter actually performs a superposition of the $\sin x/x$ function at each sample point, as shown in figure 3.7b. The reconstructed wave is shown in figure 3.7c. The resulting output signal is now a clone of the original filtered input waveform.

■ OUTPUT AMPLIFIER (g.)

Although not really part of the digital-to-analog converter circuit, an output amplifier is usually found at this point. The output waveform is raised to a line level of -10dBm or $+4$dBm, depending on the type of equipment that is interfaced with the converter.

Figure 3.6   The effects of hold time on the digital-to-analog process.

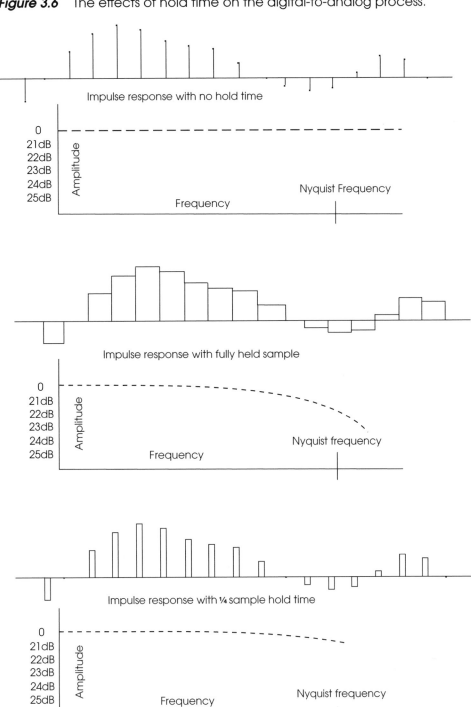

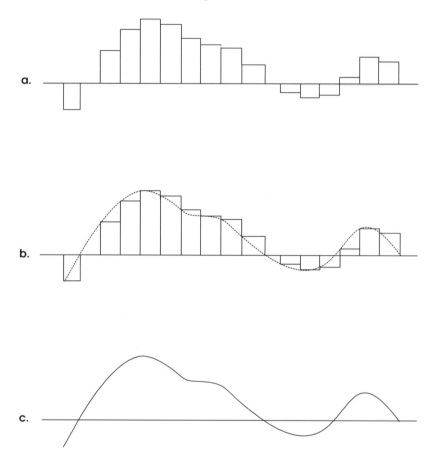

Figure 3.7 Reconstruction of the audio signal.

a.

b.

c.

■ HIGHER-BIT-LEVEL DIGITAL-TO-ANALOG CONVERTERS

Converters with more than 16 bits have been on the consumer market for some time. It is not uncommon to see compact disc players with 18- or even 20-bit digital-to-analog converters. Although it is presently impossible to derive 18 or 20 bits of actual digital data from a 16-bit storage medium, the use of the top 16 bits of a higher-bit converter can improve the amplitude resolution and linearity of the converter. Also, because the signal-to-noise ratio is determined by the number of bits in the system, a converter with more bits will be quieter. It is a known fact that digital-to-analog converters have always been at their worst near the bottom of their dynamic range. A well-designed high-bit converter may be perfectly linear down to its last 2 bits, but near this low bit level physics dictates a deviation from the desired linear response. The use of the top 16 bits of the high-bit system, maintains linearity and discards the nonlinear, lower (and unnecessary) bits.

■ OVERSAMPLING DIGITAL-TO-ANALOG CONVERTERS

As mentioned earlier, the spectrum of an infinitely short pulse has an infinite spectrum of frequencies. Because the sample pulse is not infinitely short, side bands equal in size to the base (or audio) band are created above and below the sample frequency (see figure 3.8a). Instead of looking at the signal in the traditional time domain (i.e., with amplitude on the X-axis and time on the Y-axis), we are looking at amplitude on the X-axis and frequency on the Y-axis. Note the filter response slope that is needed to accurately reconstruct the smooth waveform by preventing any of the first lower-side band from appearing in the output. As mentioned in the discussion of anti-aliasing filters, steep filter slopes cause group delay and therefore audible phase anomalies in the signal. If there were a way to move the Nyquist point to a higher frequency, we could use a filter with a gentler slope and thereby eliminate the problems. Oversampling allows this.

If we multiply the sample rate by, for example, a factor of 4, we also raise the Nyquist point a corresponding amount. If the original sample rate was 48kHz, the oversampled rate is 192kHz. The original Nyquist point was 24kHz, so the new Nyquist frequency is now 96kHz. We can then use an analog filter with a very gentle slope and nearly no phase anomalies to reconstruct the waveform, as shown in figure 3.8b. The original digital information is input to the digital-to-analog converter at the original sample rate but is output at the 4 times rate with interpolated values between the original sample points. The interpolated values are derived using a $\sin x/x$ response formula, in effect stimulating the response of the analog reconstruction process. This analog filter is referred to as a finite impulse response filter or digital transversal filter. Very high oversampling rates can even eliminate the need for an analog filter. The sampling artifacts are raised to such a high frequency that they are well above the point where they could cause problems. The recently introduced Direct Stream Digital (DSD) system uses this principle.

Another advantage of oversampling is that the quantization noise of the digital system is spread out over the entire resampled bandwidth, reducing the amount of noise in the base band by the oversampling factor. Chapter 1 showed that doubling the power increased the level by 3dB and, conversely, that halving the power lowered the level by 3dB. For example, oversampling by a factor of 4 (4× oversampling) reduces noise in the audible band by 6dB. That is, the noise is halved and therefore lowered 3dB in the base band by the first doubling and halved again by the second doubling, totaling 6dB.

Figure 3.8 The effect of oversampling digital-to-analog converters.

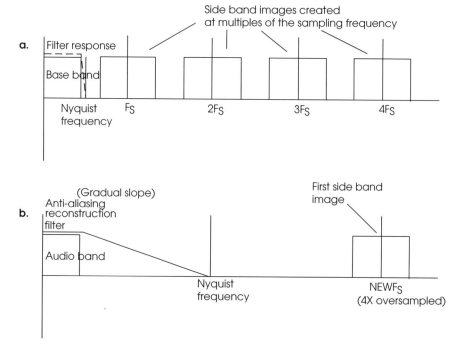

■ OVERSAMPLING ANALOG-TO-DIGITAL CONVERTERS

Having discussed analog-to-digital conversion in chapter 2 and the basics of oversampling here, let's now discuss an oversampling analog-to-digital converter.

The problems that plague the reconstruction filter also affect the anti-aliasing filter. Digital filtering, as implemented in the reconstruction process, seems to be the obvious solution. However, the oversampling digital-to-analog converter is relatively simple in contrast to the oversampling analog-to-digital converter, which requires that the analog signal be sampled and filtered before being placed in the digital domain. One solution is to sample the analog audio signal at a very high rate. This allows a very gentle filter because the Nyquist frequency is also very high. Once the signal is in the digital domain, the sample rate can be reduced and a digital anti-aliasing filter used. In fact, a digital filter is often called a decimation filter because part of its function is to reduce the sample rate. It is also known, from studies by Hauser and others, that oversampling increases the signal-to-noise ratio. In most cases an oversampling analog-to-digital converter can perform as well as or better than a standard sampling converter with a higher word length. The actual signal-to-noise ratio can be determined as follows:

$$6.02(\kappa + .5\zeta) + 1.76 = dB$$

where κ is the number of bits in the system and ζ is the oversampling octave increase. This is a dubious gain, however, because significantly increasing the signal-to-noise ratio requires very high oversampling rates.

■ ONE-BIT ANALOG-TO-DIGITAL CONVERTERS

The so-called 1-bit analog-to-digital converters are known as *delta-sigma modulation converters*. Delta modulation systems encode only the difference value between the current and previous samples. Therefore, a low number of bits can be used to represent the signal. In fact, the faster the sample rate, the less difference in quantization there is between successive samples. If the sample rate is high enough (typically 4× or even 8× oversampling), the changes between samples can be encoded by a simple 1-bit encoding system. However, as the waveform becomes more complex, the accuracy of the encoding suffers, unless the sample rate is extremely high, at which point the hardware reaches its limits.

A modification of this system is the *delta-sigma modulation scheme*. Here the value of the change (delta) from sample to sample is output by the converter but is added to the sum (sigma) of previous differences. Therefore, the entire value of the signal is quantized. Because the sample rate is many times the desired rate (44.1kHz or 48kHz), the signal can be output as a 1-bit signal but with a number of clock pulses between the slower sample rate points. That stream can be used to define the quantization level of the word. The value of the word is defined by the density or the width of the pulses between the desired (48kHz or 44.1kHz) sample points; that is, PWM or PDM is used to represent the digital word. Figure 3.9 compares PCM and PDM (PWM) encoding. The quantization level of the signal is now defined by the density of the signal, so each pulse needs only two states: high and low.

A *flash converter* is typically used for these types of systems. Such a converter is capable of very high sample rates and needs no sample-and-hold circuit but is inherently noisy, and it does carry a significant amount of quantization noise. However, the audio signal is spread out over a very wide bandwidth, so the noise level is, too. This effectively reduces the noise in the base band after reconstruction filtering. Additionally, most 1-bit systems use a technique called *noise shaping* to further reduce the quantization noise. Using the measured quantization error of the previous bit to change the current sample modifies the noise spectrum of the signal. The noise is shifted away from the audible bandwidth. As good as this may sound, delta-sigma converters, although less expensive to construct, are not the panacea they appear to be. Pulse code modulation is still the most efficient use of the binary signal, and the best efficiency results when the longest words are sent at the slowest possible rate, or two times the Nyquist frequency. This technology is typically used in an analog-to-digital converter using 1-bit modulation at high sample rates. The signal is then decimated and stored as a PCM signal, reducing the amount of space needed to store the data. On playback the signal is sent through an oversampling digital-to-analog converter. Here we have the best of both worlds.

Many digitization methods exist. Some are no longer used. Delta-sigma is a type of differential PCM. Other systems in this family are delta modulation, companded predictive delta modulation, adaptive delta modulation, and adaptive delta PCM (employed for the audio portion of Compact Disc Interactive, or CD-I). There are also floating

Figure 3.9 PCM and PWM (1-bit) conversion.

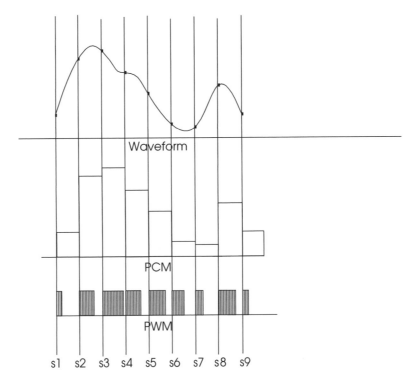

point and block floating point systems that use a mathematic scaler that is applied to the system on either a per sample or a sample block basis.

■ DIRECT STREAM DIGITAL (DSD)

A new encoding method developed by the Sony and Philips Corporations is called Direct Stream Digital (DSD) recording. The system uses a 1-bit delta-sigma modulated word converter with a sample rate of 2.8224MHz. This is 64 times the current CD rate of 44.1kHz. The professional version will sample at 128× or 5.6448MHz. Frequency response of the system is said to extend from DC to over 100kHz, and dynamic range is better than that of a 24-bit system.

The frequency response and the dynamic range are defined by the delta-sigma noise-shaping properties. As discussed earlier, filtering is needed to block any signal above the Nyquist frequency to prevent aliasing, but oversampling eases the requirements of the filter. Instead of decimating the oversampled signal into a multibit PCM signal, the DSD system directly records the 1-bit signal. Because of the high density of the samples, no decimation or filtering is needed at the input, and the signal is very analog in nature. The positive and negative values of the waveform are represented by the density of the pulses. This is called pulse density modulation (PDM). Although the DSD signal is noisy, special noise-shaping filters shift the noise up in frequency well above the audible bandwidth. The system includes the DSD analog-to-digital and digital-to-analog unit, the signal-encoding (PDM) unit, and the storage unit (PDM is similar to PWM and is illustrated in figure 3.9). In PWM the pulse width corresponds to the data word, whereas with PDM the density ratio of the positive and negative pulses correspond to the digital word. The 1-bit high-sample-rate signal can be downconverted to any current digital format, including the 96kHz 24-bit DVD standard, by simple integer multiplication and division. This is the proposed system for the so-called Super CD discussed in chapter 5.

You should now have a good understanding of the methods used to first encode and then decode digital data from and to an analog waveform. The next two chapters examine in detail the systems used for storing the digital bit stream.

FOUR

Tape-Based Storage and Retrieval Systems

In chapters 2 and 3 we looked at how the analog waveform is converted into a digital bit stream and then converted back to an analog waveform. Between these two processes is the storage medium itself. For the moment, let's consider a two-channel digital recording system, which will have a left and a right channel, a sample rate of 48kHz, and 16-bit linear PCM quantization. Adding the preambles, the CRC code, and the parity words results in at least 20 bits of data generated at each sample point. The amount of data that needs to be stored is shown as

48,000 samples $\times$ 20 bits of data $\times$ 2 channels = 1,920,000 bits per second.

The resulting data transmission rate is 1.92MHz. However, a standard analog reel-to-reel tape recorder cannot possibly record at that rate (frequency), as frequency response on magnetic tape is limited by two factors: tape speed and record head gap width. Tape speed can be increased, but then tape length would quickly become unmanageable or recording time would be very short. In fact, a tape speed of about 400 inches per second is required to record wavelengths as short as 177 microns. Thin film heads with very small gap widths are relatively easy to make, but this was not always the case. Early digital audio systems required a recorder that was capable of economically recording frequencies of around 2MHz. The answer was the video recorder, which typically can record frequencies in the 2MHz to 4MHz range.

■ ROTARY HEAD TAPE SYSTEMS

Let's look at how a typical video recorder operates. A video recorder attains effective tape speeds of about 440 inches per second by moving the tape laterally while spinning the head on a drum. The rotational rate of the head times the lateral tape speed yields an equivalent linear tape speed. However, because the head spins on a drum, it is not in constant contact with the tape, and the video signal is discontinuous. Television has taken a chapter from the film industry book and divided the video signal into fields and frames. Film uses small, still images that move past an aperture at a fixed rate of 24 frames per second. The eye-brain physiology sees this as continuous motion, as images with a perceived duration of less than 20 to 40 milliseconds are integrated. The ear also has an integration time in this range, and it is nearly impossible to discern two impulses that are spaced closer together in time than 20 to 40 milliseconds. The video industry determined that a frame rate of 30 times per second would be sufficient. This rate was further divided into 60 fields, or 2 fields per frame, on the basis of a power line frequency of 60Hz, so the spinning head records or plays one packet of information every $\frac{1}{60}$ of a second.

In the NTSC (National Television Standards Committee) television standard, 525 lines are scanned across the television screen for every frame. These are called *raster lines*. All but one of the lines are full width; the remaining one consists of two half-width scans at the top and bottom of the screen. Interlaced scanning is employed to prevent any noticeable picture flicker. With this scanning technique, every other line on the screen is skipped during the first field of the frame and then filled in with the second field during the second half of the frame. At the end of each left-to-right scan of the electron gun, the electron beam returns to the left-hand side of the screen and drops down, skipping one line, to begin the next sweep. After sweeping a complete field, the beam returns to the top-left corner of the screen to begin the first line of the next field. This return to the top of the screen is referred to as *flyback*. Just before and just after flyback, the electron beam is switched off, or blanked, and then switched back on. The time period during which it is off is called the *vertical blanking interval,* which occupies a space equivalent to 35 raster lines. You see this interval as the black bar on your television screen when the picture is rolling, but normally you do not see it. Europe uses the PAL system, which has 625 raster lines and a frame rate of 25 frames per second and therefore 50 fields. This is one of the main reasons American and European video systems are incompatible.

Some early digital systems used instrumentation recorders (machines designed to record computer data), but when Sony and Philips developed the standards for the compact disc (CD), the ¾-inch U-matic® video recorder was chosen as the specified storage device. In fact, until recently, if you had a recording that you wanted to put on CD, it had to be converted to the U-matic® format before CD mastering and pressing.

The U-matic® videotape recorder uses ¾-inch tape in an enclosed shell. The tape moves at 3 ¾ inches per second, and the head spins at 1,800 revolutions per minute. The two heads on the spinning drum are spaced 180 degrees apart. Head 1 writes field 1 and head 2 writes field 2. To play and record, the tape is pulled out of the cassette and wrapped around the drum. For fast-forward and rewind, the tape is returned to the cassette shell. Figure 4.1a shows how the tape is wound around the drum on the helical (i.e., at an angle); this is where the term *helical scanning* comes from. Figure 4.1b shows the positioning of the video record and playback heads, the video erase heads, the analog audio erase and record/playback heads, the capstan and pinch roller, the time code and control track head, and the full erase head. Time code is required when the video recorder is used for digital audio (discussed in chapter 1). Some of the newer machines have an extra set of heads that are offset 90 degrees. These heads, sometimes called *confidence heads,* are dedicated read, or playback, heads and allow a read-after-write function, which permits the digital recording to be monitored directly after recording. Figure 4.2a shows the track layout for the U-matic® system. Guard bands between each field prevent cross-talk (interference) between channels and maintain the high signal-to-noise ratio required for the video signal. A control track, which acts like a set of electronic sprocket holes, is used to phase-lock the capstan and the head drum together so that the video heads line up with the helical video tracks.

The standard audio tracks on a video recorder are analog. At best they are barely satisfactory for quality audio, so the digital audio signal is stored in the video domain. However, the digital audio data stream must be converted to a composite video signal if it is to be stored on the videotape. An ideal video signal should be flat in frequency from 1 Hz to 4.5Mhz. An FM (frequency modulated) carrier is used to avoid long wavelengths, which could cause phase anomalies, print-through, and cross-talk.

A video signal consists of several parts. The chroma signal carries the color and the luminance signal the black-and-white information.

Figure 4.1   a. Tape wrap around a video head drum; b. Tape wrap around a video head drum showing details.

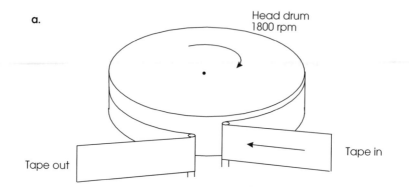

a.

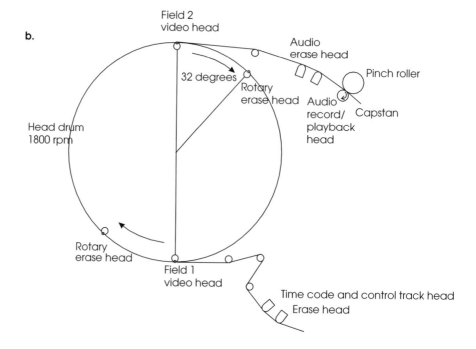

b.

Figure 4.2 a. Track layout on a ¾" helical scan videotape recorder;
b. PCM-1630 processor and associated DMR-4000 U-matic®
recorder (courtesy Sony Corp.).

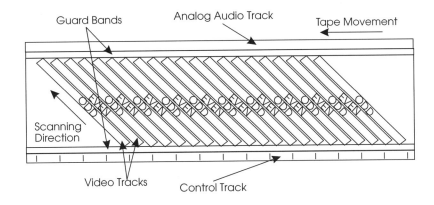

Guard Bands   Analog Audio Track   Tape Movement

Scanning
Direction

Video Tracks   Control Track

a.

b.

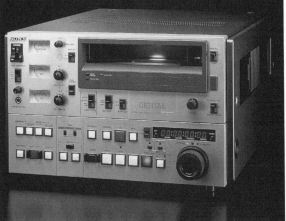

Sync signals are carried along with the video. It is beyond the scope of this book to fully discuss video technology, but you should know that when all the parts of the video signal are carried together, it is called *composite video*. When parts of the video signal (e.g., the luminance and the color information) are carried separately, it is called *component video*. Horizontal and vertical synchronization pulses must be added to the digital audio signal stream for the video recorder to record the pseudo-video signal. Also, because video recording is not continuous, data must be held in a buffer memory during the vertical interval. After video processing of the digital audio data, the video recorder is fed a signal that corresponds to NTSC standards. The binary bit stream information is stored as levels of black or white.

Early videotape digital audio storage led to the choice of 44.1kHz as the sample rate for the CD. As mentioned earlier, the Sony U-matic® system was specified by Sony and Philips as the storage medium for mastering the CD (figure 4.2b shows a Sony PCM-1630 processor and its associated ¾-inch U-matic® Recording Deck). Therefore, the sample rate had to correspond to the field rate and structure of the video signal, and because the binary bit stream emulates a black-and-white video signal, a rate of 30 frames per second rate was required. Color video runs at a slightly different rate (for more about this, see chapter 6). Blanked lines (vertical interval space) cannot be used to store data, so if we subtract 35 blanked lines from 525 lines, the remainder is 490 lines, or 245 lines per field. If two samples are stored per line, the sample rate is calculated as follows:

2 samples $\times$ 60 cycles per second line frequency $\times$ 245 lines = 29.4kHz (sample rate).

This is too low a sample rate for high-quality audio because the Nyquist point would be 14.7kHz. However, three samples per line generates a sample rate of 44.1kHz, which works also with the European standard of 625-line 50Hz video, where there are 37 blanked raster lines:

$$3 \text{ samples} \times 60\text{Hz} \times \frac{525 - 35}{2} = 44.1\text{kHz}$$

$$3 \text{ samples} \times 50\text{Hz} \times \frac{625 - 37}{2} = 44.1\text{kHz}$$

However, because the CD standard is international, the PCM-1630 CD mastering system functions only with 525-line 60Hz recorders. This allows tapes to be exchanged internationally regardless of where they were recorded. Other sample rates in use are 32kHz, used for digital audio broadcasting and long-play DAT, and 48kHz, used by professional fixed-head recorders and available also on DAT machines. Additionally, the EIAJ (Electronics Industries Association of Japan) had specified a consumer format that would record on consumer-grade color video recorders for home use. Because of the color carrier frequency, the sample rate for these systems was 44.056kHz, but such systems are no longer commonly used. The PCM-1630 system supports this rate as well.

The PCM-1630 system is being used less as mastering houses turn to *Red Book*-compliant CD recordable (CD-R), Digital Linear Tape (DLT), and 8-millimeter (mm) Exabyte tapes for transferring masters to the pressing plant. The Exabyte and DLT are discussed later in this chapter and in chapter 6.

■ DIGITAL AUDIOTAPE (DAT) SYSTEMS

The first type of storage medium designed specifically for digital audio is the digital audiotape (DAT) recorder. This recorder was originally developed for the consumer marketplace but has found its way into professional recording studios because of its ease of use and accuracy.

The ¾-inch video systems (as well as other video-based systems) in use for mastering have one intrinsic drawback. In addition to the digital audio information, other data—such as vertical and horizontal synchronization pulses, FM modulation, and control information—add an enormous amount of additional data to the recorded signal. The desire to develop small, convenient digital recorders with minimal tape consumption suitable for home use led to the creation of two small-format digital recording systems, one using a stationary-head transport system and the other a rotating-head transport, similar to current video technology. Originally, these were called S-DAT (stationary head) and R-DAT (rotating head). The superiority of the R-DAT method had established it as the sole consumer digital audio recorder until the more recent introduction of the digital compact cassette (DCC). The R prefix has been dropped, and now the unit is simply called a DAT recorder. The system has proved to be so practical that it has become a standard mix-down recording system used by many professional studios around the world. Because the DAT was designed strictly for digital audio, all the video-based information could be dropped from the signal, allowing a much greater packing density and thus reducing tape consumption. Tape is contained in a plastic cassette similar to a videocassette.

The tape, called a DAT cassette, is a high-coercivity metal particle tape. The cassette is about 2 ⅞ inches long, 2 ⅛ inches wide, and ⅜ of an inch tall and contains tape about ⅛ of an inch in width. The actual shell dimensions are 73mm wide by 54mm deep by 10.5mm high. The cassette is available in recording lengths of up to 124 minutes. The U-matic® system's record length limitation is 75 minutes, and special tape is required for that. Standard ¾-inch tape has only 60 minutes of recording time. The DAT cassette has a completely sealed structure to prevent dirt and debris (as well as fingerprints) from causing dropouts and errors in the digital signal. The tape width is 3.81mm.

The DAT recorder uses a helical scanning method of recording that is similar to that found in U-matic® videotape recorders. However, the amount of tape that is wrapped around the drum during record and playback is considerably less than in the video formats. The tape contacts the head cylinder over an angle of 90 degrees, or one fourth the circumference of the drum. Most DAT player/recorders have two heads that are used for both writing and reading data. This allows the tape to be fast-forwarded or rewound while still wrapped around the head drum with minimal tape wear or damage. This also allows the player/recorder to read the codes used for track numbering and time code during fast-forward and rewind. As mentioned earlier, conventional video recorders remove the tape from the head cylinder prior to fast-speed shuttling. The rotating head cylinder of the DAT recorder has two heads on a drum 30mm in diameter. Some newer recorders have added two additional heads for playback only. These read-after-write (confidence) heads allow the user to monitor the recording process to check for errors or other problems. However, in the playback mode the main heads, not the confidence heads, are used.

The narrow angle of contact between drum and tape means that the record or playback signal is applied to the tape only 50 percent of the time (see figure 4.3a). The remaining 50 percent of the time the signal is interrupted, and buffer memories are used to convert the continuous data stream to a noncontinuous recording format. Digital audio information is input to a memory buffer at the sample rate but is read out to tape at a faster rate. The tape travels at a speed of 8.15mm per second, or about ¼ of an inch per second. This slow longitudinal tape speed, coupled with long tape lengths in the DAT cassette, results in possible recording times of 2 hours. The head drum rotates at a speed of 2,000 revolutions per minute, which gives an equivalent writing speed of about 123 linear inches per second.

Figure 4.3   a. Tape wrap on a DAT recorder's head drum; b. Track layout on a DAT recorder.

a.

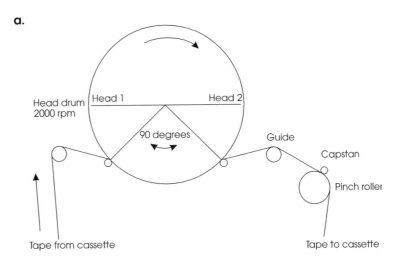

b.

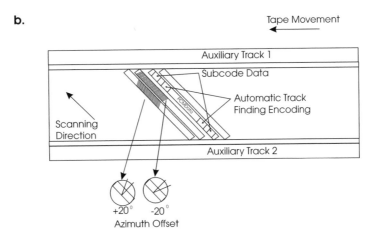

The tracks are recorded on tape without guard bands. Problems with cross-talk and tracking are avoided in the DAT format by using a method called *azimuth recording*. The tracks are tilted away from the relative vertical of the tape by an angle of ± 20 degrees. The first track has positive azimuth and the following one negative azimuth.

This condition continues for the entire tape. The length of each diagonal track is 23.501mm, yet only a portion of that length contains audio data (see figure 4.3b). Constantly comparing the azimuth angle of the pilot and sync signals between heads allows for automatic track finding (ATF). The ATF areas of each track contain a control tracking signal. This ATF azimuth type of recording allows precise tracking without the guard bands or control track signals that are necessary in video recorders. The subcode areas contain a preamble and a postamble that define, respectively, the beginning and the end of each track as well as sync and block address information. Track numbers and other information such as time code (sometimes referred to as *absolute time*) are also found here. Because the subcode section of the track is found outside the ATF and PCM areas, it can be independently recorded or edited. This allows the renumbering of tracks, replacement of start and stop identifying marks, and restriping of time code. Absolute time for the DAT can be converted to SMPTE time code by suitable code readers. Some professional machines contain circuitry allowing both write and read functions for SMPTE time code.

The DAT recording system uses a double Reed-Solomon code for error detection and correction. The signal is also interleaved, and the data are recorded across two tracks, making data retrieval possible even if only one head is functioning. The DAT system was designed to record and play back at sample rates of 48kHz, 44.1kHz, and 32kHz. However, not all DAT machines will record at all sample rates. Sixteen-bit quantization is used with all sampling rates. The DAT machine will automatically select a sample rate of 44.1kHz if a 44.056kHz digital signal is applied. This will cause a pitch discrepancy and raise the pitch by 0.1 percent. Some DATs have a so-called long-play mode, which allows 4 hours of recording on an R-120 tape. This is accomplished by changing the sample rate to 32kHz and the quantization rate to 12-bit nonlinear, thus conforming to the DAB (digital audio broadcast) standard and allowing future off-air digital recordings to be made.

■ RECORD MODULATION SYSTEMS

Figure 2.8 in chapter 2 showed that the last item in the converter chain is a record modulation circuit, which is needed to make the binary data stream suitable for recording on the specified storage medium, and although this was discussed, further explanation is needed. The output of this record modulator is sometimes referred to as *channel code* (or *modulation code*), and the type of scheme used differs with the storage medium. Prior to the modulation circuit is the analog-to-digital converter, which has a data clock that runs at the sample rate (or multiple thereof) and keeps everything in order. One of the requirements of the channel code is that the data be self-clocking to reduce jitter.

The channel coding schemes work this way. Over a specific period of time, the binary signal voltages will be the same or become reversed where, for example, a high voltage is a 1 and a low voltage a 0. These periods are called *positions* (or *detents*). Digital audio data are converted to channel bits that are output at the position (or detent) rate. The length of time between channel bit transitions is important, as are the transitions that distinguish between strings of consecutive 1s or 0s. Consecutive strings of either 1s or 0s would simply produce a direct current without indicating where one bit starts and another stops. In the example shown in figure 4.4, a 1 is indicated by a positive-going transition and a 0 by a negative-going transition. When two or more consecutive 1s or 0s appear, there is a transition in the channel coding at the beginning of each repeated bit. When a 1 is followed by a 0, there is no change. These systems allow high-density recording on the media and are often expressed as the ratio of the number of bits recorded to the number

Figure 4.4   Channel coding for record modulation.

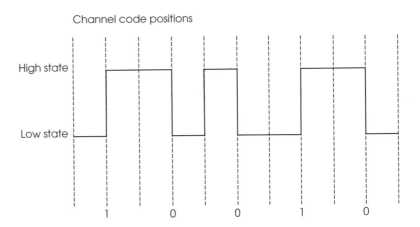

of transitions in the stream. Different encoding systems are designed and used, depending on whether the data are to be recorded or transmitted, such as for digital satellite television systems. For example, before the advent of MIDI (Musical Instrument Digital Interface), many synthesizers and sequencers "talked," that is, exchanged timing information with each other using a simple system called frequency shift keying (FSK), in which two different frequencies are used to indicate a high state or a low state. It is important to note that the transition from the high to the low frequency or state (or vice versa) defines the bit. A two-level pseudo-video signal is used to record modulate the digital audio data stream when recording on the PCM-1630 U-matic® system.

One of the purposes of the channel coding is to reduce the bandwidth requirement of the data stream. This is accomplished by sacrificing word length, but the density increase to the storage media is an order of magnitude greater because of the decrease in data bandwidth. Remember that digital bit stream density is the product of quantization (bit density) times sample rate (frequency bandwidth).

Channel codes are often named after their ratios. For example, the EFM code used by the CD is an 8-to-14 modulation code where 8 data bits are represented by 14 channel bits. Manufacturers use a code book to generate patterns that can easily be recorded, recognized, and converted by the record and playback systems. The CD uses a code book standard set by the Sony/Philips group that originated the CD. The DAT systems (discussed previously) use an 8-to-10 modulation scheme, in which 8 data bits are represented by 10 channel bits. This modulation scheme was picked because it functions well with rotary head azimuth-type recording systems.

■ MULTITRACK ROTARY HEAD SYSTEMS

Advances in digital audio coding systems and the advent of ATF made it possible to develop multitrack rotary head recording systems. Two systems are currently available. One uses the VHS format video system and the other the 8mm video format. Both systems use the high-band version (operating at higher video carrier frequencies) of their corresponding video systems. The VHS system is now probably the most popular consumer video system in use. However, its data recording capabilities are far below those of professional video recorders. On the other hand, its high-band cousin,

S-VHS, offers improved response and lower noise by operating at a higher carrier frequency. The other system, 8mm, was developed principally for handheld camcorders, and the high-band version (Hi8) of that system has been used successfully in professional video situations. These systems when used as digital multichannel recorders are often referred to as DTRS (Digital Tape Recording Systems) or MDM (Modular Digital Multitrack Machines).

Information capacity is the key element for high-bandwidth recording systems. Both S-VHS and Hi8 video systems shift the luminance signal up in frequency significantly. The standard 8mm system uses a range from 4.2MHz to 5.4MHz and the Hi8 system a range from 5.7MHz to 7.7MHz. The improvement in video resolution (to more than 400 vertical lines) translates directly to higher-density digital recording capabilities. The standard VHS system uses a carrier range of 3.4MHz to 4.4MHz and the S-VHS a carrier range of 5.4MHz to 7.0MHz. One of the main differences between Hi8 and S-VHS is that, like DAT, Hi8 uses ATF or azimuth recording and requires no control track, whereas the VHS system needs the timing pulses that the control track provides. As mentioned, both systems shift the luminance signal to a higher frequency for greater resolution. Figure 4.5 shows the frequency allocations of 8mm versus Hi8.

The rotary head digital multitrack system, based on the Hi8 video system as developed by Tascam and Sony, has eight channels of digital audio plus a subcode channel, which is used for synchronization and time code data. The helical scanning transport uses two read and two write heads. Data are written to tape as an RF (radio frequency) signal similar to the U-matic® system. The helical tracks are divided into eight channel blocks with edit gaps between them. Sample rates of 44.1kHz and 48kHz are supported, and the system uses 16-bit linear PCM quantization. Because the system writes data in a format that is incompatible with Hi8 or 8mm video, it is wise to "pre-format" the tape prior to recording. Additionally, a tape that has been used (and therefore formatted) for video cannot be used for digital audio recording.

The data blocks, or packets, are read from the tape and assembled into tracks in a buffer memory prior to output. Tascam uses two heads to read and write data into long data packets that are spread out over a large area. The system uses transparent track sharing; that is, some of the data for channel 1 may end up stored on channel 8, but the data will always play from the correct output. The first four packets are encoded and held, and the data from the next four are combined with this and then written to tape. Punch-ins and punch-outs are accomplished using digital cross-fading and

Figure 4.5   Frequency allocation for a. an 8mm and b. a Hi8 video recorder.

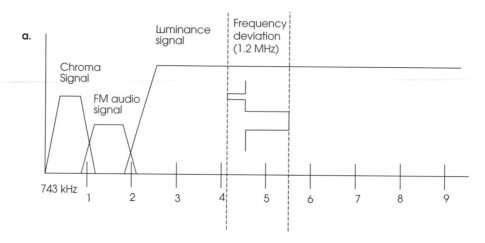

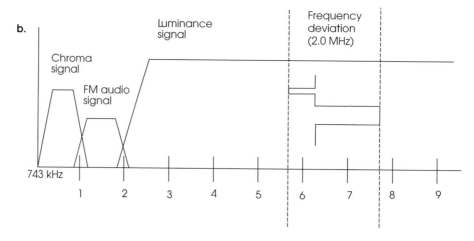

memory buffers. The Hi8 system uses a 40mm head drum and has a tape speed of 14.3mm per second, but Tascam and Sony have increased the speed to 15.9mm per second to increase tape-to-head velocity, thereby increasing frequency capabilities at the expense of recording time. Typical Hi8 machines are belt driven, but higher stability is required for digital audio, so a three-motor direct-drive transport is the norm. The higher bandwidth and greater speed stability allow a smaller minimum recordable wavelength, thereby increasing data density. This yields a recording time of 108 minutes of eight-channel recording on a P6-120 tape. The tape is a high-coercivity (1,450 oersteds) metal particle tape that gives excellent retentivity and a high output. Figure 4.6 shows a rotary head multitrack recorder with its remote control.

Twenty- and even 24-bit recording is possible on these recorders as well. Two manufacturers make add-on processors that allow high-bit recordings to be made and stored on the Hi8 DTRS system. One system (by Rane), called PAQRAT, takes the 20- or 24-bit stereo input signal from the AES/EBU digital input and divides it into four parts. These signals are then recorded on either the first four or last four tracks of the DTRS Recorder. The PAQRAT also allows the user to send the signal to all eight tracks for redundancy. With two PAQRAT devices, four-channel 20- or 24-bit recording is possible. The PAQRAT is also available for use with the ADAT system (discussed shortly). The other high-bit rate coder (by PrismSound), called the MR2024T, uses a similar approach but with different coding and channel distribution. Therefore, the two systems are incompatible. The MR2024T allows either six channels of 20-bit audio, or four channels of 24-bit recording, or two channels of 24-bit audio sampled at 96kHz with the data spread over the DTRS system's available tracks.

Figure 4.6   A Hi8mm-based eight-channel multitrack recorder (courtesy Tascam).

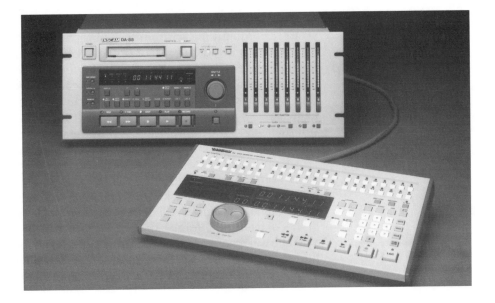

One of the advantages of this eight-channel modular approach is that several units can be chained together to increase the number of simultaneous recording channels. Three or more units can be daisy-chained to provide 24, 32, or even 48 channels. Each eight-channel unit in the chain receives a sequential identification (ID) number that allows the system controller to know that, for example, track 23 is on channel 7 of machine ID 3. Each machine has a built-in chase synchronizer, and the slave machines follow the master recorder (normally machine number 1), which contains the first eight channels. With the introduction of machines lacking redundant control functions, an economical system can be put together using one full-featured master and a number of less expensive slaves. Up to 16 units can be controlled from one remote for a total of 128 channels. Subframe accurate synchronization with other digital and video media is possible through a synchronization board that also generates and reads SMPTE time code.

The other popular rotary head digital multitrack system, the ADAT system, is based on the S-VHS transport system. The S-VHS system is the high-band version of the VHS video system common today on the consumer market. Its advantage over the standard VHS system is similar to the quality gain of Hi8 over regular 8mm video. The ADAT system records eight channels of digital audio onto S-VHS tape. It uses 64-times oversampling and delta-sigma converters (discussed in chapter 2). The system uses a standard sample rate of 48kHz with 16-bit linear quantization. Other sample rates can be used by varying the record/play tape speed. The system requires a control track on the tape and writes eight separate data blocks with each helical scan. Recording time with an ST-120 tape is 40 minutes. Therefore tape speed is three times the normal VHS standard play speed. This is required to achieve optimum packing density for the eight channels of digital audio. A RAM buffer for each track holds data until they are clocked out at the designated sample rate with all channels in sync. Prior to recording, the tape must be preformatted with control track and sync information. A proprietary sync block is added to allow up to 16 units to be combined for a total of 128 channels.

A more recent version of the ADAT allows 20-bit recordings to be made without an external bit-splitting processor. This new version, called ADAT Type II, is backward compatible with existing ADAT recordings. The new machines will detect whether a tape has been formatted in the 20-bit Type II format or in the original 16-bit Type I. The 20-bit machine will record in either the 16-bit or the 20-bit mode, depending on how the tape is prestriped by the user prior to recording. However, a Type I machine cannot play back a Type II tape. The Type II system uses delta-sigma converters and packs 20-bit audio in the same linear space as the Type I PCM 16-bit system. This allows the system to encode the difference signal instead of the entire digital word thus increasing packing density. At a sample rate of 44.1kHz, the Type II ADAT can store up to 67 minutes of eight-channel sound on an ST-180 tape.

The ADAT system uses a proprietary multichannel optical digital interface to connect multiple ADATs with fiber optic cable. The interconnection allows copying between machines in the digital domain. Copy-and-paste editing (see chapter 6) can also be accomplished between tracks by using RAM memory that is included with the larger system controller. This RAM can also be used to delay tracks up to 170 milliseconds for synchronization purposes. Track delays and other setups are stored in a data block area at the head of each tape in the system. When a tape is loaded for playback or record, the previously entered control data are recovered and implemented. The large system controller option, referred to as a BRC, also allows SMPTE synchronization, MIDI time code, and MIDI clock information. Data such as MIDI song pointers, tempo maps, and system-exclusive data can be generated and stored in the recordable data block at the beginning of each tape as well. An external sync clock-in port allows the system to be locked to SMPTE, an external word clock (at 48kHz), or composite video sync. Other optional interfaces provide AES and SPDIF interfaces (discussed in chapter 8) and chase synchronization. Figure 4.7 shows a multitrack recording system based on the ADAT S-VHS.

■ 8mm, 4mm, AND DIGITAL LINEAR TAPE (DLT) STORAGE SYSTEMS

As mentioned earlier, the PCM-1630 system is being used less for mastering CDs. Although many mastering facilities now master directly to CD-R, many send masters to the pressing plant on 8mm tape. The system was first developed by the Exabyte Corporation and is often now known as Exabyte tape. The original Exabyte transport was based on the 8mm video deck, and the tape cassette shell has the same dimensions as an 8mm videotape. However, as the requirements for digital computer-based storage became more severe, the transports and tape have been modified specifically for digital storage environments. The sound material, after editing and mastering in a suitable digital audio workstation, is encoded with a system called DDP (Disc Descriptor Protocol) and stored on the 8mm Exabyte data tape. The DDP (on Exabyte tape) was designed to emulate the PCM-1630 and

Figure 4.7   An S-VHS–based eight-channel multitrack recorder (courtesy Alesis).

DMR-2000/8000 (U-matic® transport) transfer systems used in the CD mastering system. This and the following systems are tape streaming devices with very high transfer rates. Data are transferred directly from the computer hard disk to the tape.

Another tape system, called DLT (Digital Linear Tape), is now available and has been specified for use with some DVD (Digital Versatile Disk) mastering systems. The system uses ½-inch tape in a 4.1-by-4.1-inch cartridge. Because the DDP system is not tape specific, mastering information and audio data can be stored on this system as well.

Additionally, there is a 4mm DAT system that is similar in design to the familiar audio DAT. In fact, the tapes are identical, although quality control at the manufacturing end is said to be different. This system is used primarily for backup of computer data and is not used for audio mastering purposes.

In the near future, these media may no longer be necessary for DVD or CD mastering. Several manufacturers have announced methods of sending mastered data directly to the pressing plants over Ethernet-type connections. This is the beginning of a true media-less transfer process that may filter down to the consumer level with such things as CD-quality music on demand over the Internet.

■ FIXED-HEAD TAPE-BASED SYSTEMS

Although the helical scanning method for digital recording has become the principal choice for two-channel stereo recordings, until recently inherent limitations of the system have precluded multi-track digital recorders. As we have seen, video transport based (helical) multichannel tape recorders are making inroads into the traditional types of digital audio multitrack recorders, that is, the stationary-, or fixed-, head systems. However, at this time most professional recording studios prefer the fixed-head multitrack systems. It was the advances in thin-film-head technology that permitted the design of recording heads for longitudinal recording that meet the frequency requirements of digital recording.

Two systems for fixed-head digital multitrack recording—DASH and PD—have replaced earlier types of digital multitrack tape recorders (one of which was designed by the 3M Company but is no longer made). At this time, the longevity of the PD system is in serious doubt and is available as a special order item only. The uses and functions of these two systems are similar, and an engineer familiar with the operation of a conventional analog multitrack tape recorder should have no trouble adapting to these machines. The methods of data storage, error detection and correction, and channel code and track layouts are different, and although the PD system might be completely gone in several years, each format is discussed in detail here.

Both systems offered two-track longitudinal digital recorders as well as multitrack machines but no longer do. Let's focus here on the multichannel tape recorders. Digital reel-to-reel two-track systems are practically extinct, as the DAT and the digital audio workstations have supplanted them as mix-down machines. Large-format (½-inch tape), two-channel, high-speed (30 inches per second) analog tape—combined with a noise reduction system such as Dolby SR—is still used by many studios as the mix-down format of choice.

The heads in a stationary head system are often referred to as the *erase, write,* and *read heads* instead of the more conventional *erase, record,* and *play.* Because it is very difficult for a head to perform both a read and a write function simultaneously when handling high-density digital data streams, a second read and/or write head is used in the head block of a fixed-head digital multitrack recorder. This extra head is necessary for the recorder to be able to perform synchronization or punch-in functions. Electronic cross-fading is used to smooth the transitions between old and new data during these punch-ins and punch-outs. As in analog multitrack recording, the old data are erased and replaced with new data in synchronization with the material on other tracks. To keep these transitions as smooth as possible and to reduce data errors, data buffers hold the old data at the punch-in point and cross-fade those data with the new data before sending the signal to the write head. At the punch-out point, the reverse occurs: The new data are buffered and cross-faded with the old. This electronic cross-fading and data buffering is also used to prevent data errors caused when the areas are overlapped if the tape is spliced with a razor blade. Electronic cross-fading is shown in figure 4.8.

The DASH System   The DASH (Digital Audio Stationary Head) system is one of the two professionally accepted longitudinal digital multitrack recording systems. It was developed and is supported by Sony, Studer, and

Figure 4.8   Cross-fading between the read and write heads on a digital tape recorder.

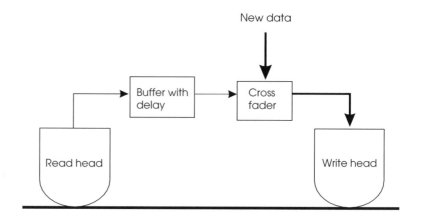

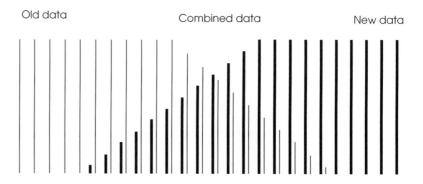

Tascam. Most DASH multitrack tape recorders have 24 or 48 channels of digital audio along with two analog auxiliary cue tracks, a SMPTE time code track, and a control track, totaling 28 or 52 tracks, which are arrayed vertically on ½-inch tape. The 48-track recorder uses the double-density DASH protocol. The second set of 24 tracks is interleaved between the first 24, allowing downward compatibility. In other words, a 24-track DASH tape will play on any of the supporting manufacturers' 24- and 48-track machines, whereas the first 24 tracks of a 48-track tape will play back on the 24-track machines, and all 48 tracks will play back on all 48-track machines. This allows maximum flexibility for interchange of tapes between studios. Figure 4.9 shows the track configuration for both the standard DASH and the double-density DASH. Each digital track is 0.17mm wide and the gap spacing within the head for each track 0.20mm. The analog tracks are slightly separated from the digital tracks to prevent the required analog bias from affecting the digital tracks.

The transport operates in the DASH-F mode at 30 inches per second when the sampling is set to 48kHz and provides 60 minutes of recording using 9,000 feet of tape, which is packed on 14-inch precision metal reels. The DASH system uses 16-bit linear PCM and has switchable sample frequencies of 48kHz, 44.1kHz, and 44.056kHz. At the lower sample rates the DASH-F tape speed is lowered from 30 to 27.56 and 26.95 inches per second, respectively. This keeps the recorded wavelengths the same regardless of the sample frequency.

Additionally, there is a high-resolution version of the 48-channel system that allows 24-bit quantization and optimal 96kHz sampling. This is accomplished by doubling the tape speed for 24-bit recording and by bit-splitting (24 tracks on 48 channels) for 96kHz samples.

The analog auxiliary tracks are primarily used for cuing purposes. The digital audio channels can be listened to only while the tape recorder is at the proper play speed. However, at times it is advantageous for the engineer to be able to hear the signal while the tape is being slowly moved by hand. The analog cue inputs are fed with signal and placed in record during the recording of the basic digital tracks. When using a typical in-line recording console, these cue inputs could be fed from, for example, the stereo monitor bus outs or a spare auxiliary bus.

The control track is used to control the speed of the transport during reproduce operations. It is recorded during the basic tracking sessions and should extend continuously all the way through the song. Because of this, the prudent engineer may prestripe the tape before the session begins. Most DASH multitrack recorders have a function called Advance Record to handle this task. The control

Figure 4.9   Track layout on a DASH 48- and 24-track digital tape recorder.

48-track	24-track	
Auxiliary track #4	Auxiliary track #4	0.35mm
Digital track #48		
Digital track #24	Digital track #24	0.17mm
Digital track #47		
Digital track #23	Digital track #23	
Digital track #46		0.17mm
Digital track #22	Digital track #22	
Digital track #45		
Digital track #21	Digital track #21	
Digital track #44		
Digital track #20	Digital track #20	
Digital track #43		
Digital track #19	Digital track #19	
Digital track #42		
Digital track #18	Digital track #18	
Digital track #41		
Digital track #17	Digital track #17	
Digital track #40		
Digital track #16	Digital track #16	
Digital track #39		
Digital track #15	Digital track #15	
Digital track #38		
Digital track #14	Digital track #14	
Digital track #37		
Digital track #13	Digital track #13	
Auxiliary track #3	Auxiliary track #3	0.17mm
Auxiliary track #2	Auxiliary track #2	0.33mm
Digital track #12	Digital track #12	
Digital track #36		
Digital track #11	Digital track #11	
Digital track #35		
Digital track #10	Digital track #10	
Digital track #34		
Digital track #9	Digital track #9	
Digital track #33		
Digital track #8	Digital track #8	
Digital track #32		
Digital track #7	Digital track #7	
Digital track #31		
Digital track #6	Digital track #6	
Digital track #30		
Digital track #5	Digital track #5	
Digital track #29		
Digital track #4	Digital track #4	
Digital track #28		
Digital track #3	Digital track #3	
Digital track #27		
Digital track #2	Digital track #2	
Digital track #26		
Digital track #1	Digital track #1	
Digital track #25		
Auxiliary track #1	Auxiliary track #1	0.35mm

1/2 inch

track uses a synchronizing pattern that contains a sector identifying mark, a control word that defines the sample rate in use, the address for data location, and a CRC code word for error protection. It is possible to synchronize two multitrack DASH recorders using their control tracks. The SMPTE time code track stores longitudinal time code for synchronization with other machines as well as transport control of auto-locate and cue functions. The larger-channel DASH 48-track recorder retains the 4 analog tracks (2 auxiliary, 1 time code, and 1 control) of the original 24-track format. The interleaved channel configuration was selected to maintain machine-to-machine compatibility within the DASH community.

The analog audio is converted to digital through oversampling analog-to-digital converters, and these data are then used to form data blocks, each containing a sync word used to identify the block, 12 data words that contain the audio information, 4 parity words that check for errors, and a CRC code word. These data blocks correspond to the sector identifying mark of the control track. Each control sector is four data blocks long and has a duration of 1 millisecond. As mentioned earlier, various modulation codes must be applied to binary audio data to achieve compact high-density data storage. The DASH system uses a channel coding scheme called HDM-1, which is an RLL (run length limited) code for packing maximum density and for reducing the bandwidth requirements of the digital data.

As mentioned earlier, it is difficult to construct a head that will read and write data on different tracks simultaneously. However, when overdubbing new material in-sync on an analog tape recorder, this is exactly what is done. To overcome this limitation, which is inherent in digital multitrack heads, the DASH system uses an additional write head. The first Write head is used for normal recording and is followed by the Read head. This allows off-tape monitoring during the recording of the basic tracks. In the sync mode the signal from the read head is delayed, and the new data are written by the second write head and applied to the tape synchronous to the data on the previously recorded tracks. Figure 4.10 shows this head layout. Note the position of the analog heads used for the cue tracks as well. As mentioned in the discussion of rotary head digital multitrack, prestriping the tape prior to recording is recommended. Prestriping records continuous control track (and time code, if desired) onto the tape to prevent discontinuities in the control track from causing a loss of sync between recorded sections of the tape.

The transport on most stationary head digital multitracks uses a servo-lock mechanism with no pinch roller. A sensor samples the tape tension at specific intervals and adjusts the current to the feed

Figure 4.10 Cross-fading between the two write heads on a DASH digital tape recorder.

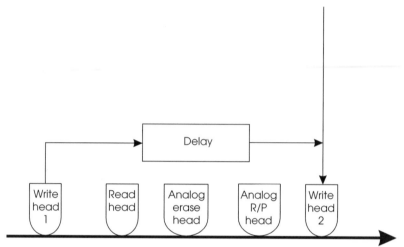

reel and take-up reel motors. Tape movement is controlled by the capstan motor, which receives information from the control track. A typical DASH transport layout is shown in figure 4.11a and a multitrack DASH machine in figure 4.11b.

The PRO-DIGI (PD) System

The other reel-to-reel stationary head digital recording system is the Pro-Digi (Professional Digital) system (commonly referred to as the PD format). It is now nearly extinct, but a number of these machines are still in use, and it is interesting to contrast the PD to the DASH. Although the two systems are incompatible, data interchange between them is possible through the use of AES/EBU digital input/output ports (discussed in chapter 8). At first glance the most notable difference between the DASH format multitrack tape recorders and the largest PD-format machines is the number of available recording channels. Although a 16-channel machine was available, most PD tape recorders allow a maximum of 32 channels of information to be recorded and replayed. With these 32 channels of digital audio are 2 auxiliary cue tracks, 2 digital auxiliary tracks, and 1 SMPTE time code track, the latter of which is used for auto-locating functions and synchronization. It is also an integral part of the block locating system in

Figure 4.11   a. Transport layout on a Sony PCM-3324A digital tape recorder;
b. a 48-track multitrack digital tape recorder (photo courtesy of
Sony Corp.).

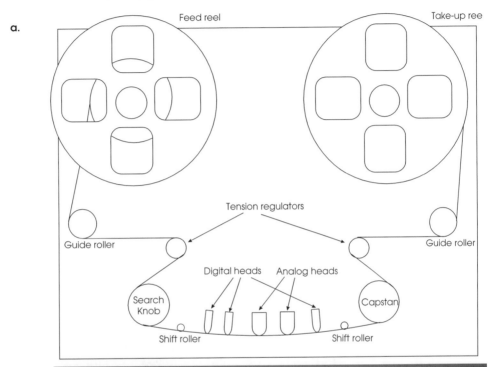

the encoding/decoding process. In addition to these tracks are 8 more digital tracks, for a total of 45 tracks on 1-inch-wide tape. The 8 additional digital tracks are divided among the primary digital tracks so that for every 8 channels of information 10 tracks are used. These extra tracks are used to store the check words of the associated digital audio tracks for the error protection system. Each digital track is 0.29mm wide, and the heads have a gap spacing of 0.27mm. The tracks are not, as in the DASH system, arranged numerically from top to bottom but are shuffled so that no two consecutively numbered tracks are adjacent to each other. However, as in the DASH format the auxiliary tracks are placed on the extreme edges of the tape, where they act as guard bands to protect the digital tracks from edge damage.

The transport, using 1-inch tape, operates at 30 inches per second, and 60 minutes of recording time are available when using 14-inch reels. The recording system uses 16-bit PCM encoding for the digital audio tracks and PWM for the auxiliary tracks. Sample frequencies of 48kHz and 44.1kHz are supported, but in the PD format tape speed is not affected by a change in sample frequencies. This means that at lower sample frequencies less data are stored on a given length of tape, resulting in a change of wavelength for any given input frequency. Speed control is achieved by locking the capstan to a reference frequency so that a control track is not required.

As in the DASH format, data from the analog-to-digital converters is used to assemble data blocks. In the PD format the data block contains a 16-bit sync word, followed by 12 data words and a 16-bit CRC code word, for a total of 224 bits within each data block. This is slightly less than the 288 bit data block used by the DASH system, which (as mentioned earlier) contains 4 16-bit check words prior to the CRC code word in each block. The check words used by the PD format are stored on the additional dedicated digital tracks. It is also important to note that the check word tracks are displaced vertically from their associated audio tracks so that the check words are not lost with the audio data in the event of a large tape dropout. The PD system uses a 4/6M (4-to-6 modulation) scheme to achieve the high packing density necessary for digital multitrack tape recorders. To allow overdubbing, the PD system uses two read heads and one write head. The basic tracks (i.e., those that have already been recorded) are played by the secondary read head (which precedes the write head) and delayed the appropriate amount so that the old data players will be in sync as the new data are written by the single write head. Figure 4.12 shows the head configurations for the PD system.

Figure 4.12   Cross-fading between the read and write heads on a ProDigi digital multitrack recorder.

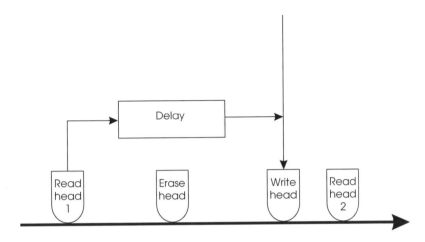

<table>
</table>

DIGITAL COMPACT CASSETTE (DCC)

A recent but short-lived digital format is the Digital Compact Cassette (DCC). Developed by the Philips Corporation from the original S-DAT designs, its major strength was that it used the standard-size compact cassette shell to hold tape. This allowed an analog playback head to be added to the transport so that the machine could play existing analog cassettes. This intentional backward compatibility was designed into the machine so that consumers could play back their existing cassette collections while recording and acquiring new material in the digital format. The tape itself is a high-coercivity metal particle tape that is the same width as analog cassette formulations. Tape speed is the cassette standard of 1 ⅞ inches per second. The concept of playing "both sides" of the tape is retained, but the cassette fits into the machine only one way. At the end of side 1 the playback head rotates 180 degrees, and the transport reverses the direction of the tape. The transport layout for the DCC is shown in figure 4.13. The tape is divided into two halves, each containing eight data tracks and a subcode track for a total of nine tracks in each direction. The playback head is designed so that the top half is dedicated to the digital tracks and the bottom half to the analog tracks. Switching between the two sections of the head, along with the ability to rotate 180 degrees, allows the deck to play any combination of side 1 or side 2 in either the digital or the

Figure 4.13   A digital compact cassette transport layout.

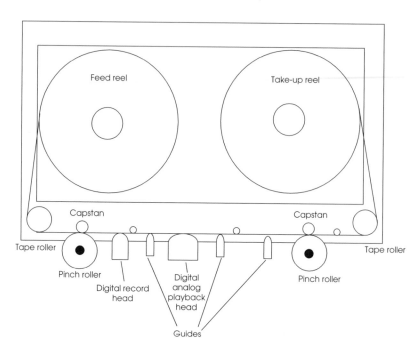

analog format. The magnetic level is so low per digital track that a special digital head using magneto-resistive technology had to be developed. Because this specialized playback head is not capable of producing enough magnetic energy across its gap width to enable recording, a separate record head is required. There is no analog record head, so the DCC deck will not record analog audio signals onto regular or digital cassette tape. Figure 4.14 shows the track layout and the playback head structure of the DCC. Even with the tiny record and playback head gaps developed for the DCC format, the amount of data produced by a full-bandwidth analog signal converted to digital audio will not fit on this medium. Tape coercivity and tape speed are the main limiting factors. For the machine to play existing analog cassettes, the tape speed of 1 ⅞ inches per second and width of ⅛ of an inch had to be maintained. This is not nearly enough landscape to record 44.1kHz 16-bit PCM digital signals.

To compensate for this, the DCC uses a data reduction scheme called Precision Adaptive Sub-band Coding (PASC), which reduces the data that need to be stored by a factor of 4 to 1. (As we will see in chapter 5, which discusses optical media storage, the MiniDisc also uses a data reduction system called ATRAC.). All data reduction

Figure 4.14 Track layout on a digital compact cassette tape and head stack.

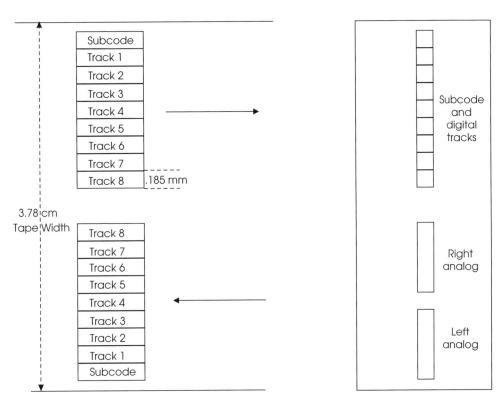

systems rely on two psychoacoustic phenomena to accomplish their task: threshold limitations and masking (both of which were addressed in chapter 1).

The purpose of data reduction systems is to encode all the audible portions of the signal with as little data as possible. PASC uses a so-called hearing algorithm that determines what information is discarded prior to data storage. This algorithm is a "perceptual model" of the human auditory capabilities. The hearing algorithm is designed to disregard inaudible sounds and sounds that are masked by louder sounds. Both PASC and ATRAC record the "perception" of the signal rather than the total signal. As we saw in our discussions of analog-to-digital conversion, using fewer bits to encode an analog audio waveform reduces the signal-to-noise ratio and increases distortions. Coding systems are designed to spread this noise and distortion over the full bandwidth of the system so that the noise and distortion are masked by their own data-reduced signal. These systems work well, and unless the listener has the original source for direct comparison, the difference may not be noticed. The largest problem occurs when a data-reduced signal must be transferred to another system or copied. For example, say that we have a DCC tape that we want to copy to another system, such as the MiniDisc. The data-reduced signal would be decoded, then sent as an analog signal to the MiniDisc recorder, where it would be reduced again, but by a different algorithm, and then stored. The sonic degradation here is unacceptable in professional applications.

The International Standards Organization (ISO) and the Motion Picture Experts Group (MPEG) have set standards for data-reduction systems. These standards were developed principally for DAB systems. The ISO/MPEG standards support sample rates of 32kHz, 44.1kHz, and 48kHz. Because different levels of data reduction are possible, ISO/MPEG specified three layers, called simply Layer I, Layer II, and Layer III. A Layer I system (e.g., PASC) divides the signal into 32 bands. The derived signals are formed into blocks and are then acted on by the perceptual coding model. The resulting outputs are recombined and requantized and then output and stored as a PASC frame. These data frames are then spread over the eight data tracks of the DCC format along with the subcode. The subcode track holds the auxiliary data, such as track number, title, and other data pertinent to the album. The DCC uses interleaved Reed-Solomon code with an approximate data redundancy of 40 percent for error protection and correction. An 8/10 modulation channel code is used.

As of this writing Philips has ceased production of the DCC system, and it remains to be seen whether another manufacturer will take over support of the units that still exist.

FIVE

Disk-Based Storage Systems

■ OPTICAL DISK STORAGE SYSTEMS

The best place to start when discussing optical disk storage media for digital audio is with the Compact Disc (CD). The CD has revolutionized the way we listen to music. A 30-centimeter (cm) disc was introduced in 1977 by Sony, Mitsubishi, and Hitachi. Simultaneously, Philips of the Netherlands was developing an 11.5cm disc. Sony and Philips combined their ideas and developed a 12cm disc with a capacity of 74 minutes, and the CD as we know it was introduced to the record-buying public in October 1982. By 1989 the long-playing record (LP) had been relegated to the back of the so-called record store. Just to refresh your memory, the LP was introduced by Columbia Records in 1948, and the first stereo LP appeared in late 1954. The LP, at its best, boasted a frequency response from 30Hz to 18kHz and a signal-to-noise ratio of about 60dB. In the stereo version, channel separation was around 28dB and harmonic distortion is 2 percent. Contrast this with a digital audio storage medium carrying a 16-bit PCM signal sampled at 44.1kHz, which (as discussed in chapters 2 and 3) has a frequency response of 10Hz to 20kHz with a signal-to-noise ratio better than 97dB, channel separation greater than 90dB, and harmonic distortion less than 0.01 percent. It is no wonder that the LP has been replaced. It is possible that another digital storage medium, the MiniDisc (introduced in 1993), may soon make inroads into the compact cassette market, the traditional format for portable music playback.

The Compact Disc (CD)

In its standard form the CD is a read-only two-channel digital audio optical storage medium. Physically, the disc is 120mm in diameter, with a center-hole diameter of 15mm and a thickness of 1.2mm. Data are stored on an area 35.5mm wide; the remaining space is used for the disc-clamping area. A lead-in area is on the inside of the disc and a lead-out area on the outside. The binary code is stored on the disc as a serial stream of pits (actually bumps) *and* nonpits. These pits are set in a continuous spiral, starting at the inside of the disc and ending at the outside. The pits are 0.5 micrometers (μm) wide and from 0.833μm to 3.054μm long. Spacing between the spirals is 1.6μm (see figure 5.1). A small, low-powered laser strikes the disc from the bottom, and the light is either reflected back to the laser or scattered. Any pit edge that has a change in its reflected or scattered status is a 1 and everything between a 0. In other words, the transitions between the pits and nonpits define the high state. The data are encoded with an EFM modulation scheme and CIRC. Subcode and sync words are included with the audio data, which are encoded on the disc at a sample rate of 44.1kHz with 16-bit quantization. The quantized data are stored as two 8-bit bytes, which are grouped into frames of 24 bytes; error correction data are added.

Subcode data carry track, timing, and index information and the sync words that define the beginning of each frame of data. A table of contents (TOC) is written in the lead-in area. The subcode from 98 consecutive frames is collected to form a subcode data block of eight data channels; each block is 98 bits long. The data blocks are called P, Q, R, S, T, U, V, and W. For audio-only CDs, only the P and Q blocks are used. The P block designates the data area and the music area of the disc. The Q block provides error detection information in the form of 16 bits of CRC code per block, address codes, and control information. Copy-prohibit and preemphasis status are defined here, as are track numbers and timings. Up to 99 tracks can be placed on a disc, and each track can have up to 99 index points. However, not all CD players can read index points. The emphasis turnover frequencies used by the CD are similar to those used by some analog magnetic tape systems. The time constants of 50 and 15 microseconds are defined with binary code in the Q block. Subcode data blocks R through W are used in other CD formats (discussed shortly). Each CD type has a standard that must be adhered to for compatibility between players. These standards were set forth in a series of color coded books by the Philips Corporation. Any manufacturer, to get a license to manufacture and produce CDs, must certify that the CD being made meets the standard for that type of disc. The CD audio standard is contained in the Philips *Red Book*.

Figure 5.1   Pit spacing, length and width for the compact disc. Note how pit length defines the repeated zeroes.

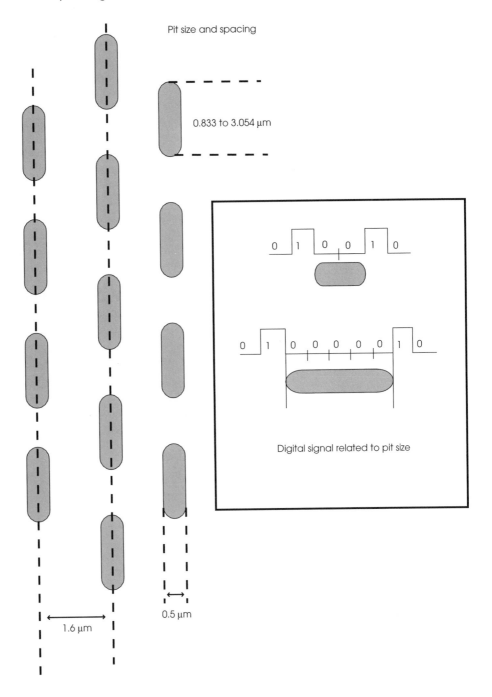

In the CD player transport, the pickup arm, which contains the laser, reads from the inside of the disc to the disc's outer edge; the rotation is clockwise. The rotational speed of the disc varies with the position of the laser, thus allowing the bit stream to output at a constant velocity. The disc standard supports 74 minutes of music but can be extended to about 82 minutes. However, discs with more than 74 minutes may not play on all CD players. A single version of the audio CD, often referred to as CD-3 is 8cm in size and holds 20 minutes of music.

The surface of the disc is overlaid with a transparent layer and the laser focused on the underlying signal layer. Therefore, dirt, scratches, and other obstructions are out of focus to the laser and are easily ignored. Figure 5.2 shows how the laser beam is either reflected or scattered as it strikes a pit and how a particle of dust would thus be out of focus to the laser. The reflected light strikes a photo detector cell and sends a stream of electrical impulses to the decoding system. The laser is guided along its spiral path by a servosystem that continuously adjusts focus and radial tracking. Specifications for the CD-DA (digital audio) are shown in figure 5.3.

Nine steps are required to make commercial pre-recorded CDs (see figure 5.4). (1) A glass plate, the size of the disc, is highly polished. (2) A special photoresistive coating is attached to the surface of the plate. (3) The coated plate is etched by a high-powered laser

Figure 5.2   Light reflected directly back maintains the 0 series while the transition scatters the beam, denoting a change. Dust particles on the substrate are out of focus.

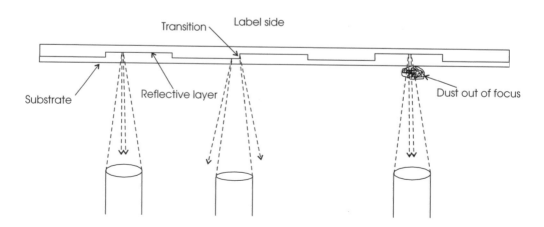

Figure 5.3   Compact disc specifications.

Signal format

Sample frequency	44.1kHz
Quantization	16-bit linear PCM
Preemphasis	Yes or No as determined by flag in Q block
Modulation	EFM
Error correction	CIRC
Redundancy	30%
Transmission rate	2.034MB/s

Disk specifications

Diameter	12cm
Thickness	1.2mm
Spindle hole diameter	15mm
Program area	50 mm–116mm
Scanning velocity	1.2m/s–1.4m/s (constant linear velocity)
Speed of rotation	500rpm–200rpm
Track pitch	1.6μm
Pit size	3.054μm–8.833μm

beam and the intensity of the etching beam modulated by the digital audio bit stream. (4) The photo layer is developed, revealing the pits and nonpits. (5) The surface is silvered for protection and then (6) nickel plated. (7) This metalicized master is used to make "mother" plates, which are then used to make stampers. (8) The stampers are used to make the plastic discs themselves by either injection molding or compression molding. (9) The signal surface of each disc is coated with vaporized aluminum and then sealed with a protective transparent plastic layer. These steps, and many of the specifications listed in figure 5.3, are identical to those used for the different types of CD in use today.

CD-ROM   The CD read-only-memory (CD-ROM) format is used principally for computer data storage and distribution. The CD-ROM can store 450 1.44-megabyte (MB) high-density computer floppy disks. A CD-ROM player identifies this type of disk as different from an audio-only CD by the Q subcode channel block. Because most CD-ROM drives include the ability to play audio-only CDs, discs with audio, instruction sets, and still- and full-motion video are found in the computer

Figure 5.4 The compact disc pressing process.

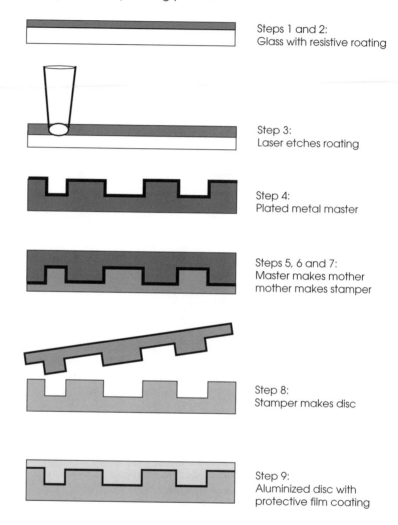

Steps 1 and 2:
Glass with resistive roating

Step 3:
Laser etches roating

Step 4:
Plated metal master

Steps 5, 6 and 7:
Master makes mother
mother makes stamper

Step 8:
Stamper makes disc

Step 9:
Aluminized disc with
protective film coating

game market. In fact, books (especially those on musical subjects with musical examples) are increasingly being published in CD-ROM format. For example, a CD-ROM about Mozart could have still pictures of Mozart, an instrumental score, digital audio, and even video clips from the movie *Amadeus.*

The frame size used in the standard CD is really too small to handle all the data required by the CD-ROM format. Therefore, each 98 of the 24-byte data frames are summed into sectors to increase the workable data block size for graphics and video. A typical CD-ROM has a storage capacity of about 650MB. The digital audio on the CD-ROM is processed with the same EFM scheme as the regular audio-only CD; however, synchronization information and time and track data are stored in each sector as well as in the Q subcode channel.

The CD-ROM also has a mode byte that tells the playback system which type of data are on the disc. Mode 1 is used principally for computer software data, such as databases and program information. Mode 1 uses an additional amount of error correction in conjunction with the standard error correction found on audio-only discs. This extra correction ensures that essential computer data are not lost or interpolated. Mode 2 is used principally for video and graphics (but for audio as well) and uses the additional bytes (required for extra error correction in mode 1) for user data. The CD-ROM standard is defined in the Philips *Yellow Book*.

Extended Architecture CD-ROM

The Extended Architecture (XA) CD-ROM allows computer data, data-reduced audio and video data, and still-picture data to be stored on one track. This format is an extension of the Yellow Book mode 2 standard. It allows data from modes 1 and 2 to be interleaved on the same track (similar to the CD-I format, which is described below) and so is often referred to as a "bridge" format between CD-ROM and CD-I. The CD-ROM/XA format is defined in the Philips *White Book*.

Compact Disc Video (CD-V)

Compact Disc Video (CD-V) contains digital audio and full-motion video (this should not be confused with the video CD, which is a subset of the CD-ROM standard). The CD-V is a combination of an audio CD and a video laser disc and can store about 6 or 7 minutes of a video with audio plus another 20 minutes of audio only, making it ideally suited for the music video market as presented by MTV. The video portion is stored on the outer part of the disc in analog (as on CLV and CAV laser discs) and the music on the inner portion as digital audio. Therefore, CD-V players can play audio-only CDs, and an audio-only player can output the audio part of a CD-V. The discs are found in both the NTSC and the PAL/SECAM video formats. As in CLV and CAV laser video discs, the audio portion of the music video is modulated with the analog video as a composite video signal and encoded on the disc as a combination pit track. On playback the audio is demodulated and sent to the digital-to-analog converter.

The specifications for CD-V are in the Philips *Blue Book.* Compact disc videos as of this writing, are rare.

Video CD

The video CD, often incorrectly called CD-V, is a version of the CD-ROM standard. It uses a data-reduction system called MPEG (Motion Pictures Experts Group) and can hold full-length motion pictures along with high-quality audio. It plays from a conventional CD-ROM drive and allows the user to watch movies on the computer monitor. The standards for video CD are defined in the Philips *White Book,* the original specification of which was developed for the karaoke market.

Compact Disc Interactive (CD-I)

Compact Disc Interactive (CD-I) is also a subset of the CD-ROM standard. Like CD-ROM, it can combine text, video, graphics, and music. Audio can be 16-bit PCM data or 8-bit ADPCM (adaptive delta pulse code modulation). In the ADPCM scheme, the sample and quantization rates determine the frequency response and dynamic range of the music. Its three modes—hi-fi, mid-fi, and speech mode—roughly correspond in fidelity to a standard LP, an FM broadcast, and an AM broadcast, respectively. Interactive playback is possible because up to 16 tracks of monaural music with a 74-minute length can be encoded using data-reduction schemes. The CD-I audio modes are shown in figure 5.5. (Various video modes are available as well.)

As audio and video quality increase, the amount of total available time decreases. The video data are stored digitally and as such can be played back following either the NTSC or the PAL/SECAM standard. The system uses interleaved data and allows for real-time switching between sectors, which may contain different types of data. Therefore, user selection of different sectors is possible while the disc is playing. For example, in a children's learning program, by selecting among certain icons or figures from the main image screen, a child can be taken to branches of the main program by way of software, and each branch will have its own audio and video information. The CD-I standard is set forth in the Philips *Green Book.*

Photo CD

The Photo CD was designed to display high-quality still pictures. Images from conventional color negatives (print film) or color positives (slide film) are scanned digitally and stored on the Photo CD,

Figure 5.5 Compact Disc Interactive audio formats.

Audio Modes	Encoding Type	Sample Rate	Quantization	Possible Channels
CD-audio	PCM	44.1kHz	16 bit	1 stereo
Hi-fi (A)	ADPCM	37.8kHz	8 bit	2 stereo 4 monophonic
Mid-fi (B)	ADPCM	37.8kHz	4 bit	4 stereo 8 monophonic
Speech	ADPCM	18.9kHz	4 bit	8 stereo 16 monophonic

which typically can hold as many as 100 photographs. Discs can be played back on dedicated Photo CD players (and on standard CD-ROM drives, as long as the appropriate software is used).

Digital Versatile Disk (DVD)

The newest member of the CD family is the Digital Versatile Disk (DVD), originally referred to as the digital video disk because it was initially designed to store full-length motion pictures. Members of the DVD family include DVD-video, DVD-audio (standard not specified yet), DVD-ROM, DVD-R (WORM, or write-once-read-many), and DVD-RAM (Rewriteable). The DVD player plays audio-only CDs as well. Although similar in appearance to the audio-only CD, the DVD may contain two sides of data, each holding 4.7 gigabytes (GB), compared with the audio-only CD's 680MB. Dual layer DVDs can hold 8.5GB on a single side, for a total of 17GB on the disc. One of the differences that allows the DVD to hold this much data is a change from the standard CD in pit size and track spacing. Recall that the audio CD has $0.83\mu m$ of minimum pit length and $1.6\mu m$ of track spacing. The DVD uses $0.4\mu m$ of minimum pit length $0.74\mu m$ of track spacing. In addition, the wavelength of the red (instead of infrared) laser is shorter. A conventional CD player's infrared laser emits light at a wavelength of 780 nanometers (nm), whereas the DVD player emits a red laser with a wavelength of 650nm. There is also a DVD-ROM that uses a laser wavelength of 635nm. The system uses a type of EFM channel coding called EFM Plus. The DVD also has a more robust error correction system, called RS-PC (Reed-Solomon Product Code), than the standard CD. The DVD specification calls for two layers when necessary. On the first pass, the laser focuses on the deeper layer and then, as the second layer is selected, refocuses to read the nearer, semitransmissive layer. A buffer memory on board the player prevents data interruptions while switching layers. It is said that DVD can deliver quality approaching the D-1 digital video standard, but not all experts agree on this.

Encoding the massive amount of video and audio data is accomplished by using MPEG-2 compression. The MPEG set a series of compression standards (data reduction) for video that are used for graphics and videos in many digital graphics formats. The MPEG-1 reduces the data frame by frame, whereas MPEG-2 uses motion-compensated data reduction. The coding scheme analyzes the video picture for redundancy. Only the difference between frames is coded so that the redundant data are not recorded in full form, thus allowing far lower bit rates. The DVD uses a component digital video compressed to bit rates of up to 10MB per second rather than the bit rates of 216MB per second used by the D-1 digital video system. The disc also has space for five channels of digital sound. Movies can carry digital stereo sound or one of the multichannel formats that provides discrete left, center, right, left-rear, and right-rear sound. A common subwoofer channel is included in the Dolby AC-3 system, which is a multichannel surround playback system with multichannel information is matrixed into the audio tracks. This is often called 5.1 encoding (L, C, R, LR, RR, and low-frequency channel).

The DVD-audio may lend itself to the so-called super CD format, which might expand the sample and quantization rate of the existing audio-only CD format and thereby expand frequency response and dynamic range. Both 96kHz 24-bit systems and 1-bit oversampling systems (with sample rates in the 2.8MHz range) are being considered by several standards groups. One important consideration is that the "new" audio CD standard should retain compatibility with existing CD players. Although the new DVD players will play standard CDs, most of the first-generation machines cannot read CD-R discs (discussed next). Some second-generation players will play CD-Rs either by including a second laser or by changing the wavelength of the existing laser when a non-DVD disc is sensed.

Recently, a super CD format with downward compatibility was proposed by the Sony/Philips group. The Super Audio Compact Disc is a hybrid mastered with Direct Stream Digital (DSD) technology. It is a double-layer CD with the top layer adhering to the CD-A *Red Book* standard (see figure 5.6). As in the DVD, the dual layer disc is accomplished by superimposing a semitransmissive layer, which will hold up to 4.7GB, on the CD density reflective layer, which will hold 780MB. The CD-A layer is transferred using Super Bitmapping

Figure 5.6   Super CD.

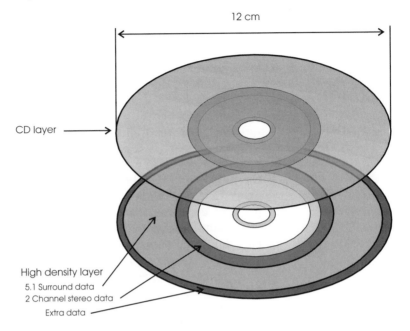

12 cm

CD layer

High density layer
5.1 Surround data
2 Channel stereo data
Extra data

(SBM) so that many of the advantages of the DSD process are maintained in the normal 16-bit 44.1kHz mode. If you recall, DSD uses a very high sampling rate and delta-sigma conversion to achieve extremely wide bandwidth and dynamic range. The second layer of the CD contains a clone of the original DSD 2 channel data along with the surround-sound mix also in DSD format. The proposed system contains the six-channel surround data as full bandwidth signals. The current DVD surround 5.1 standard uses five discreet signals of full bandwidth audio with a band limited subwoofer channel. There is also an area on the second layer of the disc for extra data such as text and graphics. Players will contain two lasers: one with the current 750nm wavelength for playing the CD-A layer and other standard CDs, and a 650nm wavelength pickup for playing the high-density layer. Because the shortwavelength pickup is the same as that used for the DVD, it follows that these special players will play nearly any format CD or DVD. Total music time for each layer of the Super Audio CD is 74 minutes. Additionally, there is a new copy protection system called Digital Watermarking designed to prevent piracy. Using a technique called pit signal processing (PSP), an image is watermarked into the disc surface. This image is nearly impossible for pirates to duplicate, and a lack of the image or the corruption of it will alert merchandisers to illegal copies. The watermark technology also contains disc bar codes and other irremovable information embedded on the disc. This CD will allow the listener to choose either standard CD audio, high-resolution two-channel sound, or six-channel surround sound.

Compact Disc Recordable (CD-R)

Compact disc recordable (CD-R) is a WORM system that allows a specifically designed recorder player to record digital audio information on a CD. The data cannot be erased or recorded over after the initial writing. When the disc is completed, it can be played as many times as needed on a standard CD player. This medium is a pregrooved blank disc enclosing a photochemical dye or a thin metal film usually made of tellurium. A digital bit stream with EFM encoding modulates the writing laser. The laser strikes the dye or metal film, changing its reflectivity. On playback the pickup reads the changes in reflectivity as the pits or nonpits of a conventional CD. The disk is recordable and playable on the CD-R recorder player only until it is "fixed up" or finalized, at which time a permanent TOC and subcode data are written. The disk can then be played back on an ordinary player. Some systems write a temporary TOC so that the disk can be played back and new material added later, after which (during the fix-up stage) the permanent TOC is written. Erasing data is not possible, and once the disk is full, there can be no further recording. Capacities of 550MB and 650MB are available, giving 63 minutes and 74 minutes of record/play time, respectively.

CD-Rs can be written in the Track-at-Once (TAO) mode or the Disc-at-Once (DAO) mode. In the *Red Book* standard, a CD is produced by first writing its table of contents in the TOC area, then writing the music in the data area. This is a continuous process and cannot be stopped until all data are transferred without ruining the disc. In the TAO mode, individual tracks are written and connected by link blocks, and the TOC is written after all data are recorded. This is the *Orange Book* mode. CD-Rs that are written for use as a source for glass mastering of commercial CDs are required to be written in the DAO mode. *Orange Book* (TAO) discs need to be converted to either a *Red Book*–compliant disc, a PCM-1630 master, or a DDP Exabyte master, usually at the client's expense.

Some confusion exists regarding the length of music time available for a CD-R. The general rule is that digital audio requires about 10MB per minute for a stereo audio data stream of 16 bits sampled at 44.1kHz. The CD-R writes audio (and other) data at 75 sectors per second. The number of bytes per sector depends on the kind of data written. For audio, one sector equals 2,352 bytes; for data, one sector equals 2,048 bytes. One disc manufacturer states on the back of its CD-R media product, "The nominal 650 Mbytes is the capacity when the medium is recorded in the ISO 9660 Mode-1" (i.e., the data mode). Other manufacturers of discs targeted for the music market simply state their capacity as 74 minutes. A little math shows that 74 minutes of stereo audio at 2,352 bytes per sector times 75 sectors times 60 seconds yields 783,216,000 bytes. However, because a megabyte is 1,048,576 bytes (1,024 kilobytes [KB], or 1,024 ×1,024), the amount needed for 74 minutes of audio is 746.89MB. This is the amount of space needed on a computer hard disk for 74 minutes of music. On the other hand, data with 2,048 bytes per sector uses only 650.39MB. Therefore, although audio requires 10MB per minute in stereo, a 650MB ISO 9660 CD-R will hold 74 minutes of audio.

The CD-R also has a power calibration area (PCA), where a trial recording is made when the disc is inserted in the machine to calibrate the laser's power level. This is necessary because of dye characteristics and temperature variations. The two major types of dye in use today are cyanine and phthalocyanine, the former green in color and the latter more golden. Additionally, there is now a bluish-silver-colored dye that is a hybrid chemical mixture. There is also a program memory area (PMA), where a temporary TOC is written. If the player/recorder does not find a TOC in the lead-in area (LIA) (i.e., before the disc is finalized), it will search the PMA for the temporary TOC.

As this medium becomes more affordable, it too may challenge the portable music supremacy of the audio compact cassette and could lead to the early demise of the MiniDisc format as well. The CD-R conforms to the Philips *Orange Book* standard prior to the fix-up stage and to the *Red Book* standard thereafter.

CD-R systems are found as stand-alone devices containing the drive, analog-to-digital and digital-to-analog converters, line-level electronic circuitry, and control systems. These stand-alone units usually have analog (+4dBm or −10dBm) and digital (AES/ EBU and/or SP/DIF) inputs and outputs that are accessible on the back of the units. The CD-R drives can also be found as peripherals for computer-based systems either in digital audio workstations (discussed in the next two chapters) or in computers for CD-ROM implementation. The drives can be internally mounted in the computer or can be external. The internal models rely on the computer's power supply and are internally cabled to the host's SCSI (Small Computer Systems Interface) adapter, whereas the external models have their own power supply and case and are cabled to the host by an SCSI cable. Either way, the drives are assigned a unique SCSI device number. For digital audio this requires that the host computer have analog-to-digital and digital-to-analog converters available or attached to the system. Many of the newer systems use the fast SCSI-2 protocol interface, a standard that is also used on some of the stand-alone units. There are also IDE-based CD-R drives, but for audio purposes the SCSI versions are preferable. Figure 5.7a shows the front and the remote control of a stand-alone CD-R machine; figure 5.7b shows the rear. Note that the rear panel has connections for two types of digital connections (dis-

Figure 5.7   a. The front panel of a CD-R machine with its remote control; b. the rear of the same machine showing the SCSI-2 interface as well as the AES/EBU, S/PDIF, and analog inputs and outputs (photo courtesy The Marantz/Superscope Corp.).

a.

b.

cussed in chapter 8), balanced analog inputs and outputs, and two SCSI connectors with a SCSI address selector. Two SCSI connectors are required because the unit may or may not be the last in the chain of seven possible devices.

The stand-alone CD-R provides maximum flexibility in the digital audio workstation system (discussed in chapter 6). This unit can be used as a stand-alone recorder/player using the CD recorder's internal analog-to-digital and digital-to-analog converters and as such will record audio-only CDs. Two machines can be connected for high-speed ($2\times$) copying of audio CDs, CD-ROMs (mode 1), CD-Is, and CD-Vs. And with the unit interfaced to a digital audio workstation (which might also have an internal SCSI CD-R drive), copying, mastering to two discs at once, and other combinations are possible. Another feature of stand-alone CD-R machines is that subcode data from the DAT (i.e., track number IDs) are sent to the CD-R and reconfigured as P and Q data before being recorded on the CD as track and index numbers.

DVD Recordable (DVD-R)

The DVD recordable (DVD-R) is the DVD equivalent of the CD-R and is a WORM system. Its discs are readable (depending on material content) on DVD-ROM and DVD-video players. Initially, the 120mm DVD-R holds nearly 3.95GB of data on a single-sided disc and 7.9GB on a dual sided one. The standard also calls for an 80mm disc that will hold 1.23GB of data. The DVD-R uses the smaller pit size and track spacing of the read-only DVD and a red laser with a wavelength of 635nm. The disc is pregrooved (as in the CD-R) and uses a dye polymer recording layer. Dual layer recording is not currently implemented. A recorded DVD-ROM uses a new file system called UDF Bridge, which provides for both the newer Universal Disc Format (UDF) and the ISO 9660 system used by the CD-ROM; therefore, it provides backward compatibility with older systems.

Magneto-Optical Media

Recordable erasable optical disks are becoming used in both the professional and the consumer areas. The Sony PCM-9000 is considered by some to be the logical successor to the PCM-1630 CD mastering system, and the MiniDisc was designed to replace the compact cassette in portable situations. The PCM-9000 uses a proprietary recording format but essentially does the following. As magnetic material is raised beyond a certain temperature (called the *Curie point*), its magnetization dissipates. As the material cools, it takes on the magnetic polarity of any magnetic field applied to it. The magnetic field, derived from the digital data system and applied by the write head, then orients the spot on the disk in a north or a south polarity corresponding, respectively, to a 1 or a 0 of the digital bit stream. Once the temperature of the spot falls below the Curie point, the magnetic polarity is permanent until the medium is heated once again (see figure 5.8). The erase laser dissipates the magnetism of the spots prior to recording, and the recording laser/ coil combination sets the polarity. The polarity of the material is then read by a laser using the Kerr principle, by which the polarization plane of light is rotated slightly by a magnetic field (see figure 5.9). The reflected light passes through a polarizing filter, and the intensity of the light passing through the filter determines the bit state. The professional version of this system uses a 133mm single-sided disk and is capable of storing over 100 minutes of recorded audio data. The disk is sealed against air to prevent corrosion of the magnetic material. Coding is a variation of the EFM code used by the CD and the MiniDisc. However, the system is designed to be used with up to 24-bit quantization and supports sample rates of 48kHz, 44.1kHz, and 44.056kHz. Error correction for the system uses a varia-

Figure 5.8   The recording system for the MiniDisc.

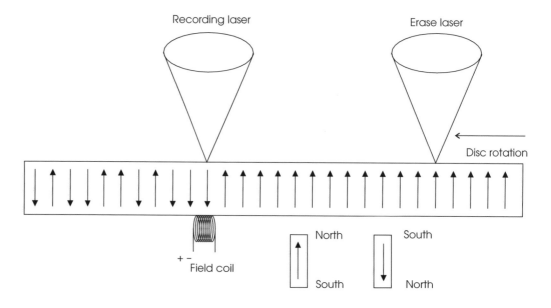

Figure 5.9 The playback system for the MiniDisc.

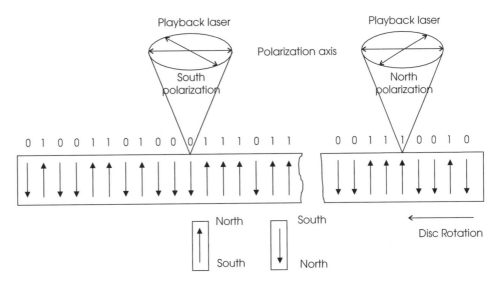

tion of the CIRC, and data are recorded with constant linear velocity. With 20-bit quantization at a 44.1kHz sample rate, the disk can store 80 minutes of stereo material. Using 24-bit resolution, data storage is reduced to 65 minutes. The recorder/player is designed to be used with an electronic editing system similar to the one described for U-matic® recorder/players in chapter 6. The system is capable of editing precision at the sample level. The disks are pregrooved, and address information is pre-recorded. This address information (which negates the need for prestriping) is then used to generate SMPTE time code data for editing and synchronization. Figure 5.10 shows a magneto-optical recorder/player.

At 20- and 24-bit quantization levels, the unit is designed to be interfaced with an SBM processor unit in the recording and CD mastering stages. The SBM processor outputs the 16-bit data standard required by the CD. *Super bitmapping* is a form of data reduction that uses processing algorithms based on the human hearing model. In addition, it uses noise-shaping techniques to move quantization noise outside the audible range. The SBM system reduces noise by as much as 24dB, shifting the noise from the 3-to-5kHz area, where the ear is most sensitive (refer to the Robinson and Dadson curves in chapter 1), to an area where the ear is less sensitive. The noise does not go away; rather, it becomes less audible. The SBM system also reclocks the signal prior to output to reduce timing errors or jitter.

Figure 5.10   A professional magneto-optical recorder (courtesy Sony Corp.).

MiniDisc   The MiniDisc, introduced by the Sony Corporation in 1990, is a miniature version of the magneto-optical disk system. It operates on the same optothermal principal but is smaller in size. However, to achieve the same time capabilities of the CD, the MiniDisc uses a data-reduction scheme called ATRAC (Adaptive Transform Acoustic Coding). The disc is 64mm in diameter and encased in a rigid protective case, much like a 3½-inch computer floppy disk. The MiniDisc's specifications are shown in figure 5.11.

The ATRAC compression system reduces the data by a factor of 5 to 1. It divides the 16-bit 44.1kHz signal into 512 bands in the frequency domain using a fast Fourier transform (FFT), shown in the inset in figure 5.12. The spectrum is divided into narrower bands in the low frequencies than in the higher ones. ATRAC uses a psychoacoustic algorithm that takes advantage of the masking effect and the threshold of hearing. One of the major problems of any data-reduction system is multiple-generation copies. This is not true of the super bit mapping system because the audio data end up as a 16-bit quantized signal on the final storage medium. With DAT and other linear PCM encoding systems, the data are literally cloned, and the copy sounds identical to the original. However, with ATRAC (and PASC, used for the DCC), the reduced data, when played back, are converted to a 16-bit data stream and the missing data interpolated. Therefore, if the interpolated bit stream is copied, it is reduced by

Figure 5.11 MiniDisc specifications.

Recording/Playback time	74 minutes
Size	72mm × 68mm × 5mm
Diameter	64mm
Thickness	1.2mm
Track pitch	1.6μ
Linear velocity	1.2–1.4m/s

Audio Specifications

Channels	2 (stereo/monaural)
Frequency response	5–20kHz
Dynamic range	105dB
Sample frequency	44.1kHz
Compression	ATRAC
Modulation	EFM
Error correction	CIRC
Laser wavelength	780nm
Recording system	Magnetic field modulation

another factor of 5 to 1. The data losses from the compression algorithm are additive, and each generation has less data than the preceding one, causing a loss of fidelity. The data-reduced recorded signal cannot be copied because it is not accessible prior to interpolation.

Thankfully, the ATRAC algorithm has been improved on since the introduction of the MiniDisc. ATRAC 1 was introduced with the MiniDisc player in 1993. It was noisy and reportedly had a metallic sound. ATRAC 3, introduced in 1995, was much less noisy because dynamic filtering was added, and the sound was considered "pretty close" to DAT. ATRAC 4.5, the current incarnation, is said to be equal to DAT in fidelity. Pre-recorded MiniDiscs without the magneto-optical coating exist, and these are manufactured like the CD.

The MiniDisc itself is composed of several layers of a polycarbonate substrate, a magnetic recording layer, a dielectric layer, a reflective layer, and a protective layer. The recordable disc is pregrooved with a wobbling pattern that represents address information. During recording, the MiniDisc system uses a recording head (the magnetic overwrite head) and a laser to simultaneously erase and record. The laser heats the magnetic layer to the Curie point, permitting it to be remagnetized by the recording head. For playback the same laser at a lower intensity reads the disc. The reflected laser light rotates (or polarizes) according to the magnetic field orientation and is recognized as either a change state or not a change state. This is similar to the magneto-optical disk system shown in figures 5.7 and 5.8.

Figure 5.12   A block diagram of the MiniDisc record and playback system.

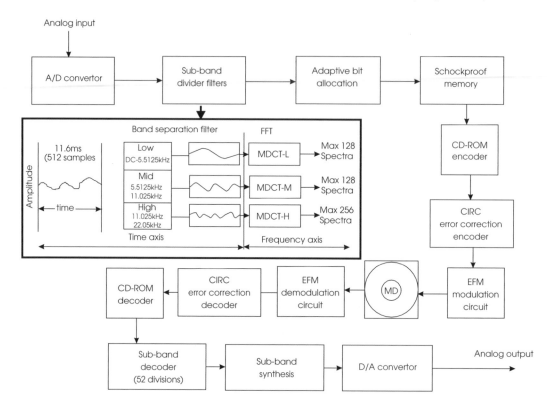

Because the recordable MiniDisc is always updating its TOC in the record mode, it is easy to edit existing recordings by changing the TOC. Audio may even be divided between two segments on the disc with, for example, 2 minutes at one point and 6 minutes at another. The MiniDisc player's read-ahead buffer makes the connection between the two segments seamless as the selection is played. This buffer system also allows the user to program the TOC to insert, delete, resequence, split, and join sections of music with no audible problems. This acts like a miniature digital editor.

Multichannel MiniDisc Recorders   During the heyday of analog recording, several companies introduced multichannel recording systems based on the compact cassette format. These so-called porta-studios recorded four tracks of audio onto the familiar cassette format tape but at higher speeds. The higher speed allowed improved high-frequency response and extended dynamic range. With the advent of the MiniDisc, these same companies have introduced MiniDisc multitrack recorders that use MD-DATA discs. These discs, originally designed for computer applications, differ from the audio-only variety in the way the cluster and sectors are recorded on the disc. The MD multitrack system allows simultaneous recording on four tracks, with a maximum time of 37 minutes per track. The systems will also record 74 minutes of material on the MD-AUDIO pregrooved disc. Some units will allow access to the ATRAC encoded material for bouncing of tracks to other locations on the same disc. But, as in the two-channel recorder versions, the ATRAC data-reduced information is not available externally.

The MiniDisc specification, as developed by the Sony Corporation, is contained in the *Rainbow Book*. This specification is an adaptation of the CD-A *Red Book,* CD-ROM *Yellow Book,* and CD-MO *Orange Book.*

CD Rewriteable (CD-RW)

The compact disc rewriteable (CD-RW) is a phase-change medium similar in makeup to the MiniDisc. However, the system uses a 120mm CD-sized 650Mb rewriteable disc. The CD-RW's drives are designed to read current CD-ROM and CD-R discs. However, because the method of reading and writing is a phase-change system, CD-RW discs cannot be read on standard CD, CD-R, or CD-ROM drives. The CD-RW discs are readable by DVD-video and DVD-ROM players because of the shorter-wavelength laser. The CD-RW format is specified in the Philips *Orange Book, Part III.*

DVD-RAM

The DVD-RAM is a rewriteable DVD format with the capability of 2.6GB of storage per side. It uses a 120mm disc contained in a cartridge to protect it from dirt. The specification declares that it will be compatible with DVD-video and DVD-ROM. However, one manufacturer has stated that the drives will have two lasers, one with a 650nm wavelength, the other with a 780nm wavelength. Therefore, the unit will support all DVD and all CD formats, including CD-R and CD-RW. The DVD-RAM uses phase-change technology and will be available in single- and dual sided versions for a total storage space of 5.2GB. Data are recorded on both the grooves and the lands; that is, the areas between the pregrooves of the disc will also be used for data. Currently, no plans for a dual layer version exist.

■ MAGNETIC DISK STORAGE SYSTEMS

We have just discussed many of the permanent and temporary disk-based storage media for digital audio. However, the most prevalent one in the digital audio workstation is the so-called hard disk. Don't ask why, but traditionally the word *disk* associated with a computer ends with a *k* and *disc* associated with a CD or a MiniDisc with a *c*. From the early stages of computer development, systems have had an internal readable and rewriteable storage area. The earliest personal computing systems used cassette tape drives with a system called the *Tarbell interface,* but these were soon superseded by the so-called floppy disk drives. These removable storage media were soon supplemented with a hard drive. The hard drive (or disk) is where the data reside. It is interesting to note that the Tarbell interface could sustain data transfer rates of only 600 bits per second. (More on transfer rates later.)

Early 5 ¼-inch single-sided floppies were capable of storing 360KB of data. Do you remember how much space is required for a minute of digital audio in stereo? At a sample rate of 44.1kHz, a quantization of 16 bits, plus error correction codes and so on, two-channel (or stereo) digital audio requires about 10MB per minute of storage, or 5MB per minute per track. Therefore, on a standard floppy you could store 2.7 seconds of stereo material—not enough even for a commercial or a news sound bite. Floppy disks did develop into units capable of more storage. In fact, 3 ½-inch floppies with 1.44 MB of storage are common. There is even an experimental 2.88MB floppy, but the falling price of CD-ROMs may preclude this development. Even so, 2.88MB is only about 17 seconds, and transfer rates are below 90KB per second.

On the other hand, it is possible to find hard drives today of 4, 6, and even 9 or more gigabytes of storage. Transfer rates (how fast a device can output information) on a modern hard disk range from 1MB per second to as much as 4.2MB per second; 1.2MB to 1.6MB per second is average. For digital audio, the minimum is about 1.3MB per second. Digital interfaces (discussed in chapter 6) have much higher rates because of their channel coding schemes. Remember, the CD has a transfer rate of about 1.5MB to 2MB per second, depending on the format (CD-A, CD-ROM, CD-I, and so on), and the DVD has a rate of 10MB per second.

Let's take a quick look at the makeup of a modern hard disk. Although it is called simply a hard disk, it contains several platters, or a number of disks stacked together on a common spindle. Each platter has 2 sides—8 platters with 16 sides is a common configuration. Like the floppy, each platter is coated with a magnetic coating of specially treated ferric oxide (similar to that found on magnetic tape). Each platter side has an electromagnetic read/write head and is controlled, collectively, by an actuator arm. The drives are sealed so that no alignment or cleaning is required. Each surface is divided into a series of concentric rings, each called a *track*, and a series of pie-shaped wedges, each called a *sector.*

When head 0 is over track 322 on platter 1, side 1, heads 5, 6, 7, and 8 are also over track 322 but on platters 3 and 4, respectively. The heads all move together and cannot move independently. The relationship of the head to track 322 on platter 1, side 1, and all other track 322s is the same. This vertical alignment is called a *cylinder.* Figure 5.13 shows a platter divided into tracks and sectors; also shown are an actuator arm and a head. Figure 5.14, showing a stack of platters with multiple heads attached to an actuator arm, illustrates the

Figure 5.13   A computer hard disk showing sectors and tracks.

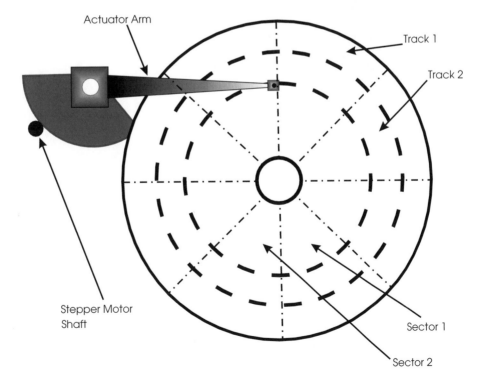

Figure 5.14   A computer hard disk stack showing the concept of cylinders.

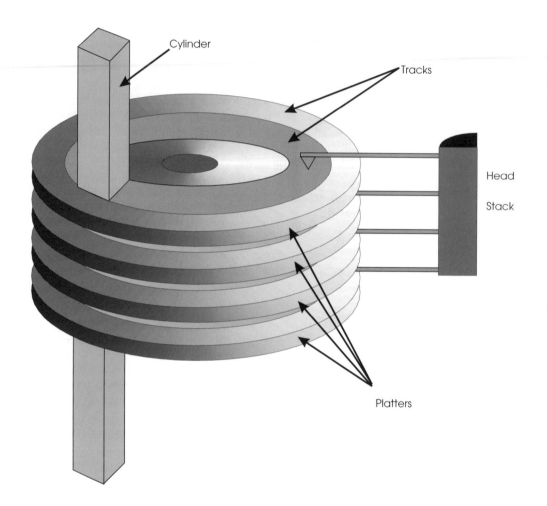

concept of cylinders. The location of a data block (holding 512 bytes) on a hard disk is addressed by head, sector, and cylinder. Hard disks use modified frequency modulation (MFM), also known as Miller coding, to increase storage density.

Another important factor for a hard drive used in digital recording is *seek time* (or *access time*), which is the time it takes to position the head over the correct cylinder and track. Actually, the head movement is the seek time, and the time it takes the disk to rotate to the correct sector is called the *latency period*. For digital audio a seek time of 20 milliseconds or less is required. Most hard disks today have seek times between 8 and 14 milliseconds.

Because a hard disk is essentially free running (i.e., not synchronized to anything), a method to link the time on a recording and the data location on the disk is needed. The SMPTE/EBU time code, locked to the audio signal, is used to build a TOC for the disk that associates the SMPTE address with the physical block address of the disk. Although data are stored sequentially when possible, bad sectors or blocks on the hard disk may cause data to be stored discontinuously. The address table tells the disk where to seek the next sequential audio data block when it is called for. The time code can be generated internally by the digital audio recording system or carried along with the digital signal input, as in the AES/EBU interface (discussed in chapter 8). Disk addresses are compiled and stored in an index also so that a piece of audio, when called for, is addressed to the system by its file name and time code. Because the data are pulled off the disk discontinuously, the data are fed to a RAM buffer that collects and then outputs the data at a constant rate.

One of the main drawbacks of the hard disk is its immobility. The fact that data must be loaded onto the drive prior to editing or processing can be time consuming. Also, when the project is finished, the data must be downloaded to a portable medium, such as CD-R, for delivery to the client. Then the disk often will need to be reformatted or defragmented to prepare a clean slate for the next recording. A highly fragmented disk (i.e., where data blocks are placed on a disk nonsequentially) can slow seek times and cause glitches or blanks in the data output.

Removable Hard Disks

Removable magneto-optical disks have been around for some time. They are fast but expensive. Several types of removable magnetic hard-disk drives have recently become available. The disk platters are contained in a cartridge that slides in and out of the transport. Early cartridges had a capacity of 100MB, or 10 minutes of stereo digital audio. The SCSI version of these drives had a data transfer rate of about 1MB per second, barely enough for digital audio. A 1GB removable cartridge drive was developed that used a fast SCSI-2 interface and had an average transfer rate of 5.5MB per second and a seek time of 12 milliseconds. More recently, a 2GB version was introduced, and larger cartridges and drives may soon follow. The drives are perfectly suited for digital audio workstations, several manufacturers of which have certified the drive for use in their systems. Cartridges cost about half as much as a reel of 24-track digital audio tape, and the cartridges are said to have a shelf life of 10 years or more. This allows the digital audio engineer to work on a project, remove the cartridge, work on a different project, and return to the original project later. When the project is finished, the cartridge can be given to the client, who may archive it or return it later for more work on the same data.

There are also frames and carriers that will hold a conventional SCSI or IDE hard disk. These systems have a switch or a key that powers down the drive and allows it to be removed and replaced with another. These "hot swappable" drive carrier systems will hold drives 12GB or greater in size. Both of these removable disk systems may well change the face of the digital audio editing suite.

SIX

Digital Audio Editing

■ TAPE-BASED EDITING SYSTEMS

Editing is the process of either rearranging the order of program material for an album layout or replacing errors in the performance with corrected portions. Accomplished analog editors (engineers with razor blades) could edit individual notes from one performance to another as long as the transitions between notes were clean. It was very difficult, if not impossible, to make inaudible edits in, for example, a sustained french horn note. Unless the editor managed to exactly match the waveforms at the edit point, an audible glitch would occur. This was all done by ear because no visual representation of the waveform was available, and if an error were made, the engineer would need to repair the incorrect edit before proceeding with the desired one. Tape speed also influenced the available precision of the edit. Much more space exists between any two notes at a tape speed of 30 inches per second, than at 15 inches per second, so the music sometimes would be "bumped up" to a higher tape speed for editing, but at the expense of another added generation of noise, to perform the desired edit.

In the digital domain, such edit problems do not exist. In fact, although razor blade editing can be accomplished on digital reel-to-reel tape if great care is taken, it is certainly not the preferred or most accurate method. Oil from fingers causes dropouts, which increase the error rate and tax the error-correcting system. Control track discontinuities can also cause problems, and the familiar technique of rocking the tape back and forth across the head to find the splice point is not possible using digital data. At the slow speed involved, the decoding system simply does not function, and the operator cannot listen for the splice point. Reel-to-reel digital recorders solve this problem by providing a pair of channels onto which analog audio information is recorded in synchronization with the corresponding digital audio tracks. This is often done during tracking by dumping the monitor mix to these "cue tracks." As mentioned, the razor blade edit is quite likely to interrupt the normal sequence of sync word (or preamble), audio data, CRC code, and parity information. The razor is not always able to sever the tape at precisely the correct spot to preserve the proper sequence of data flow, so a momentary data discontinuity may occur from which the system will take a relatively long time to recover. As a result, the splice will create a noisy transition as it momentarily disrupts the orderly flow of data. This may be correctable by error protection and correction schemes (mentioned in chapters 2 and 3), but a severe enough discontinuity could create a momentary audio mute.

Various systems have been designed to make razor blade editing possible. The data discontinuity is sensed, and an electronic cross-fade interpolates data to smooth out the transition across the splice. A major difference in the splicing block in razor blade editing is that the cut is made exactly vertical rather than at an angle, as used with analog tape. Because the flux change across the magnetic head gap is electronically cross-faded, a butt splice (90 degrees) is preferable because all data on all tracks are now severed at the same place.

The best method of editing digital audio information is electronic editing. Tape-based digital audio editing systems were derived from editing techniques used in the video industry. These techniques are used principally for two-channel digital audio recorded on professional U-matic® videocassettes and DATs. Unlike traditional razor blade editing, in which a collection of tapes may be played back and spliced together on a single tape recorder, the electronic editing process for helical scan digital systems requires two machines: a player and a recorder. The takes, which are to be assembled into the master tape, must be reproduced on the player and copied onto the recorder one at a time. Most helical scan electronic editing systems use SMPTE/EBU time code as the reference for edit points (refer to the discussion of time code in chapter 1).

Now let's see how an edit is accomplished. For example, we want a final master that is edited from sections of three separate takes (see figure 6.1). Note that the master will begin with take 3, followed by a portion of take 2 and then by take 1. Two types of videotape-based electronic editing are used: assembly editing and insert editing. *Assembly editing* is used when no existing control track or SMPTE

Figure 6.1   The assemble edit process.

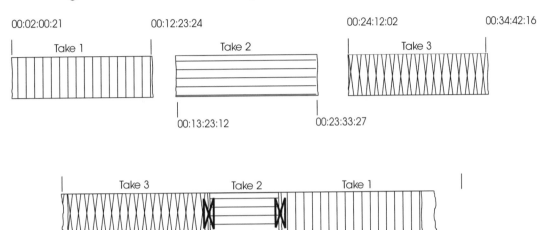

time code exists on the target tape. *Insert editing* is used when continuous control track or SMPTE time code is already recorded on the tape and new material might be placed between two segments of existing material. Assembly editing edits the video signal (digital material) and audio signal (analog material and time code) simultaneously. The control track on the videocassette (containing digital audio) is edited at the same time so that the head switching lines up properly with the helical recorded video tracks. Insert editing allows the video signal (digital audio material) and analog audio tracks 1 and 2 (SMPTE/EBU time code recorded here) to be edited independently or simultaneously and all signals referenced to the existing control track. In digital editing, the assemble mode is generally used only when a song or master tape needs to be extended, as a break in the control track signal could occur. Normally, the tape that is to be used for the assembled master is prestriped with SMPTE time code (audio track 2) and control track signals prior to the edit session and then the insert edit mode used. This ensures continuous time code and control track, both of which are essential for proper mastering onto CD, DAT, or other digital media.

We begin by copying (dubbing) the beginning of take 3 (from figure 6.1) onto the recorder. The transfer should start before the first note and continue for several seconds beyond the required edit-out point. Then take 2 is cued up on the player and stopped a few seconds before the edit-in point, where it is to begin replacing take 3. Simply transferring take 2 onto the end of take 3 will not work. The odds of making an accurate and undetectable transition from one take to the other at the proper spot are remote. However, all video-based digital audio electronic editing systems have some form of rehearse mode, in which the edit takes place electronically. The editing procedure begins by listening to the end of take 3 from the recorder (not the player) and executing an edit-out command at the appropriate moment. This command marks the selected edit point where take 3 ends and transfers several seconds of audio from both sides of the edit point into a buffer memory. The contents of this memory can now be reviewed at regular or slow speeds so that the edit point can be modified or confirmed. Next the edit-in point of take 2 (the next segment) is selected from the player. Again, several seconds of program on either side of the proposed edit are loaded into the buffer memories in the editing system, and the engineer may adjust or confirm the actual point. Now the edit is played in its entirety. Some systems do this from the buffer memories, whereas others play the previously recorded material and switch, at the edit point, to the new material. Again, the edit point(s) may be adjusted repeatedly until the transition is perfected. A cross-fade between the two segments is required, and different durations can be auditioned to achieve the optimum edit. Cross-fade times from 1 millisecond to 1 or more seconds are often available to make the transition as smooth as possible (similar to varying the angle at which the analog tape would be razor edited). Most digital editors are able to simulate the traditional tape-rocking search for an edit point. The contents of the buffer memory can be "rocked" back and forth at any play speed, usually by manipulating a rotary knob designed to create the illusion that a piece of analog tape is being moved back and forth across a playback head.

Once the edit points are located and confirmed, the electronic editing process begins. The master recorder rewinds to a convenient "pre-roll" location well ahead of the edit and begins playing. As the edit point approaches, the player transport (containing take 2) starts in synchronization with take 3 on the recorder. SMPTE time code is used as a reference to synchronize the two machines together. At the appropriate moment, the recorder switches from the play mode to the record mode, erasing the final moments of take 3 (thus the importance of rehearsal) and replacing it with the new material from the player (take 2). Take 2 continues to be dubbed onto the recorder through the next edit-out point, after which the recorder stops and the process begins again with the next take. In our example, this is take 1. This continues with succeeding edits until the end of the editing project is reached.

The electronic editing procedure just described may require some rethinking of traditional editing techniques, especially for engineers who are accustomed to working with a razor blade and splicing tape. For example, once the electronic edit has taken place, the new material must continue to be dubbed onto the master recorder until the next edit point is reached (no skipping ahead to the next edit), and the editing process often takes considerably longer than the razor blade method. However, no razor blade editing can match the accuracy or smoothness of an electronic system. Some systems require the engineer to review the previous material up to the next edit point before proceeding, and this is always useful. A final review of the edit to make sure that the flow of the music is not interrupted is always a good idea. An advantage of this assembly/insert edit system is that even if the edit is not correct and some data have been copied incorrectly, the edit can be re-created because the original material (i.e., what is on the playback machine) is still intact. Figure 6.2 shows a video-based electronic editing system that is designed for use with the PCM-1630 or PCM-9000 digital recording systems. This system will interface with reel-to-reel DASH machines as well. However, a digital editing system utilizing two 24-track DASH machines and an electronic editor may be cost prohibitive.

■ DISK-BASED EDITING SYSTEMS

With the proliferation of personal computers and the attendant fast-paced developments in software, it did not take very long for the audio industry to adopt this technology. New RAM storage systems and other disk-based storage media are appearing in the control rooms of major recording studios at a high rate.

The principles for recording digital audio with disk-based systems are not much different from those of recording digital audio using either helical scan recorders or longitudinal digital systems, in which the digital bit stream is written to either an optical or magnetic storage disk. One limiting factor is simply the storage capability of the disk itself. External Winchester disk stacks have been successfully used by some manufacturers, whereas others are using the hard disks found in personal computers. The maximum recording time is limited simply by the storage capacity of the disk divided by the sample rate and quantization and again divided by the number of tracks required. With many systems, the engineer decides how many tracks are necessary for the required work and how to apportion the disk storage resources accordingly. A system of this type may be initially purchased with a minimum amount of storage time, and as the

Figure 6.2   A professional digital editor (photo courtesy of Sony Corp.).

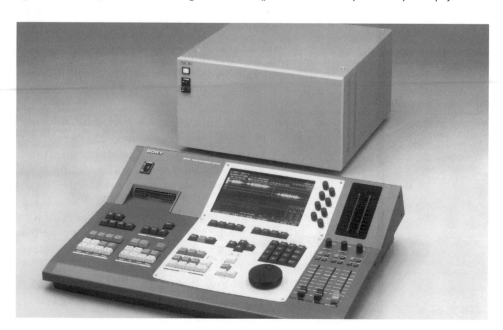

fortunes of the studio increase, additional blocks of storage time may be added by supplementing the number of disks in the system. Recall that 5MB are needed at a sampling rate of 44.1 kHz with 16-bit quantization for each minute of digital track time.

Another limiting factor of these systems is the amount of time necessary for downloading and uploading data. For example, if a series of tracks are recorded, overdubbed, and mixed down within the system, the storage will be tied up until the material is downloaded (in real time) to some permanent storage medium. Conversely, if existing material needs to be loaded into the system for processing, editing, or even further overdubs, the time required can be extensive. This can create problems in busy studios where clients demand minimum turnaround times. Newer systems now have the ability to write data at accelerated rates to CD-R or Exabyte tape. Uploading from either analog or digital tape media is still in real time, but some systems accommodate so-called background processing, which allows the user to load in and/or load out a new project while working on the edits of the current project.

Most of these systems write digital audio data to magnetic disks. Hard disks may be either outboard, as external self-powered devices, or internal. These disks can be easily erased and prepared for new data, after the desired material is downloaded, by a simple format-type command. Some older systems use WORM optical disks. In this type of DRAW (direct-read-after-write) system, data, once written, are permanently encoded into the disk, which is encased in a protective envelope that is inserted into the front of the recorder (like a video-cassette) to keep it free from dust and debris. A benefit of this system is that the material is recorded permanently and cannot be accidentally erased by an errant format command. Once the data are stored onto the disk, removing or restoring the material is as simple as inserting the carrier into the machine. However, a large project can use quite a few disks, and once the session is over, the material might not be used again. An optical disk can hold a substantial amount of data, often as much as a magneto-optical disk can.

Editing with a Hard-Disk System

The advantage of hard-disk systems becomes readily apparent with electronic editing. The editing systems and software that are now available have made electronic editing possible for the small studio. Personal computers, coupled with specified hard-disk drives, can edit digital audio data with proprietary software, just as a text file is now edited. The audio data are treated as a file that can be moved, joined with new material, replaced, or deleted almost as easily as editing a letter on a word processor.

In most systems, the file can be auditioned as the edit points are determined. The edit point can then be displayed on a screen and visually edited with a mouse or other pointing device. The cross-fade times can be varied, and the edit can easily be previewed and changed prior to actually performing the edit. These data are stored by the computer in an edit decision list (EDL), which is simply a set of pointers or addresses that tell the editing software where to find the data on either side of the edit point. When the edit command is given, the computer assembles the data either in memory or on an unused portion of the hard disk by using the first material up to the edit-out point, followed by the second material with the appropriate cross-fade between the new and the old. It is possible to completely preassemble an edit list for an entire selection before telling the editor to proceed. Even then, the original material remains unchanged in case a different edit decision needs to be made. This is often referred to as *nondestructive editing.* The terms *on-line editing* and *off-line editing* stem from this practice. Developing an EDL by manipulating data in a non–real time (i.e., not play speed, but piece by piece) is referred to as off-line, or nonlinear, editing. Switching data "on the fly" (i.e., in real time, as in some video systems) is referred to as on-line editing.

In some systems, when the play command is issued, the system writes a new file containing the material in the cross-fade, stores it on the disk, and writes a pointer in the EDL. In other systems with fast processing, the cross-fade is simply re-created in real time each time the pointers jump from one section to another. The completely edited selection can then be downloaded to one of the permanent removable storage media (e.g., DAT or other digital storage media discussed in chapter 5).

Further developments along these lines have created the so-called digital audio workstations (DAW), which combine recording and editing functions with digital mixing and signal processing. A DAW includes a personal computer and the manufacturer's hardware and proprietary software that is installed on the host computer. These DAWs may well be the recording studios of the future. In chapter 7 we discuss the digital editing and mastering process of a two-channel stereo piece of material and then examine the process of multitrack recording and mixdown on one of these systems. First, however, let's examine the computer systems that we may find in a typical environment.

■ PERSONAL COMPUTERS AND DAWs

A large amount of processing power was needed in the earliest days of computer-based digital editing. The first successful system of this type was developed by one of the pioneers of digital audio, Dr. Thomas Stockam. His system used a mainframe computer (called a VAX PDP-11/45) from Digital Equipment Corporation. The computer itself was roughly the size of a small refrigerator and the disk stack nearly as large. It was kept in a temperature- and humidity-controlled dust-free environment, and the operator communicated with it from a remote terminal consisting of a screen and a keyboard. Data were loaded into the system from large reel-to-reel computer tape transports. For that time this system, called the Soundstream Editing System, was remarkably quick and accurate.

As computers evolved, desktop systems became available. The first of these personal computers (PCs) used all text-based input systems for which two distinct *operating systems* were developed: CP/M and DOS. An operating system is the set of instructions used by the computer to translate the user input to machine (binary) language, which is used to process the data. (It is beyond the scope of this book to delve into operating systems and machine language, and many books on the market address these specific topics.) The PCs from IBM and the so-called PC *clones* (i.e., those licensed but not manufactured by the original developer) quickly found a niche in the business community. These computers used processors designed by Intel and others and were assigned numbers that defined their place in the ever-advancing technology. One of the earliest was the 8086, which was followed quickly by the 8088 and the 286. However, these were too arcane and complicated for many people to use without their having full knowledge of computer technology.

Another company, Apple, developed a more user-friendly desktop system that used a graphical user interface (GUI) and a pointing device called a mouse. Apple's early machines evolved into the Apple Macintosh computer, which has become one of the mainstays in today's music industry. This system features an intuitive GUI with pull-down menus for issuing commands. One of the earliest Macintosh processors was the 6800 followed by the 68020, 68030, and 68040. These processors, designed by the Motorola Company, included a math co-processor on the central processing unit (CPU) chip, whereas the early Intel products used a separate chip for math processing. As the popularity of the Macintosh machine soared, especially in the creative arts fields (e.g., graphic design and publishing), the original developer of DOS (Digital Operating System) introduced a GUI for the PC. This system from Microsoft, called Windows, attempted to duplicate the user-friendly working environment of the Macintosh. However, as the Macintosh platform was introduced earlier and was easier to use, it became the preferred system for developing music-processing software. An early entry in this field was the sequencer, which stored MIDI data on a disk, where it could be manipulated on a screen using the mouse and keyboard commands. As processors and hard disks became more powerful, it became possible to take the output of an analog-to-digital converter, convert it to computer data, and store the resultant binary code on the hard disk. As the PC GUI became more like the Macintosh system, digital audio systems for the PC began to develop as well.

Many people now feel that the two operating systems can equally perform the required digital audio functions, although some are still more comfortable on the Macintosh. The serious student of digital audio should be proficient on both platforms. In fact, now it is the DAW software that determines the functionality of the DAW system, much more so than the platform or the platform's operating system. However, some inherent differences should be mentioned.

■ DESKTOP COMPUTERS

Apple initially used a SCSI bus for communicating between internal hard disks and the CPU, whereas PC manufacturers used an IDE (Integrated Drive Electronics) interface. Both the SCSI and the IDE interface have their advantages and disadvantages. One of the disadvantages of the IDE system is that the drive must be located internally and connected with a multistranded ribbon cable. Until recently, large internal hard-disk drives (i.e., larger than 350MB) could not be located inside the desktop computer frame. Also, because digital audio takes so much storage space, the larger drives were usually located externally. This led to the predominance of the outboard SCSI drive for hard-disk digital audio storage. Now, internal IDE and SCSI drives easily exceed the 1GB range, but the external SCSI drive is still preferred. Drives in the range of 4GB to 9GB are available, but beyond that it is more practical to daisy-chain multiple drives. The SCSI standard allows up to seven external interconnected drives for each SCSI interface in the system. Internal IDE drives are used in some systems for the archival storage of digital data, and IDE interfaces for the internal CD-ROM drive are common. However, at this time most CD-R and DVD-R drives are SCSI only.

The market has recently seen in influx of removable medium-sized hard drives based on the Winchester disk technology. It is interesting to note that the original Soundstream System used Winchester-type drives, but they were not removable. One of the new removable disk systems has a capacity of 2GB and seek times and transfer rates equal to and even exceeding some SCSI drives. The media are reasonably priced, the transports are available as internal or external units, and the units work with either the Macintosh or the PC platform. This could well be the storage medium that the digital audio editing community has been waiting for, as it would allow the studio to book back-to-back editing sessions without the upload/download problem.

Another difference between the Mac and the PC is where and how the interface cards are implemented. A small computer usually consists of a motherboard that contains the CPU, BIOS (Binary Instruction Operating System) chip set, the keyboard interface, and master circuitry for the system. Additionally, a power supply provides voltage for the systems and the peripheral hardware, such as the internal disk drives (both hard and floppy), internal tape drives (for archival storage), and CD-ROM drives. The motherboard contains slots for memory SIMMs (single in-line memory modules) or DIMMs (double in-line memory modules) and interface cards. Accessory interface cards are used to attach external peripherals such as monitors. Modems, SCSI interfaces, and sound cards are inserted into these slots also. The Apple Macintosh, prior to the PowerPC (discussed later), uses a slot standard called NuBus for its cards, whereas the PC uses the ISA system. Because of different lengths, connector configurations, voltages, and many other differences, these cards are not cross-system compatible. This difference is critical because most DAWs do not rely on the computer's CPU to process the audio but rather have multiple DSP (digital signal processing) chips on a proprietary interface or adapter card. These cards also usually contain the interconnections between outboard digital hardware, such as analog-to-digital and digital-to-analog converters. End users need to either choose the platform and then investigate the DAW hardware available for that platform or pick the DAW system that is best for their application and use the specified platform.

■ RISC TECHNOLOGY

A more recent turn of events is the change in processor technology to a RISC (Reduced Instruction Set Computing) CPU internal operating structure. Following the early PC-based Intel 286 processor was the Intel 386, 486, and the Pentium. These, and the Motorola 680x series (68020, 68030, and 68040) used in early Macintosh computers, were all CISC (Complex Instruction Set Computing) technologies. All the Motorola chips had built-in math co-processors, whereas the early Intel chips provided a separate socket for one. Because of the complexity and density of the digital audio bit stream, a chip without a math co-processor was at a distinct disadvantage for DAW use. In fact, most manufacturers specified a built-in co-processor as a requirement for the host computer. The 386 and 486 series of chips were available with or without on-chip math co-processors and were designated with a DX suffix if there was an onboard processor and with an SX suffix if there was none. Therefore, a 486DX chip had a co-processor, whereas the 486SX did not. All Pentium chips have the math co-processor.

As the Motorola 680x chip series reached the limits of their computing power, Apple, IBM, and Motorola developed a new type of chip for personal computers called the RISC processor. This technology had been used in mainframe computers but was never developed for desktop use. This new set of CPUs was introduced by Apple in the

PowerPC, and these micro-architecture chips are designated the 600 series. The first version was the 601, and versions include up to the 604. The latest version is called the G3. The RISC chips are also found in some PCs, although the Pentium, Pentium Pro, and Pentium II still dominate sales.

The RISC technology offers the advantage of speed. The circuitry for CISC chips is extremely complex. The instruction set uses long blocks that vary in length, and this length causes a loss of speed. The RISC instruction set uses short blocks of identical length, and it uses out-of-order execution. Both PowerPC chips and the Pentium family also contain internal cache memory on the CPU chip to increase processing speeds. All this extra speed translates to additional digital audio processing capabilities, such as equalization, dynamic processing, and sample rate conversion in real time.

Another change that occurred with the advent of the more powerful Pentium and RISC CPUs was a difference in the type of accessory interface slots in the computer. The NuBus and ISA slots, being principally 16-bit cards, were limited by the speed at which they could access the rest of the computer system; NuBus was the faster system, and an ISA version called VLB (Vesa Local Bus), using 32-bit architecture, was adopted by the PC industry. Local bus refers to the fact that the card in the VLB slot has direct access to the motherboard systems rather than going through the polling and queue system of the ISA bus. The PC can have a combination of either ISA and VLB slots or ISA and the new PCI bus. At this time the VLB bus is nearly extinct. The PCI card is a local bus, 32-bit card with the size and power requirements of a 16-bit ISA card. With the addition of an extended slot, 64-bit cards are now appearing. The PowerMac series uses PCI slots exclusively. The PCI was supposed to be an industrywide standard, but not all manufacturers adhered to the complete standard, and so the interchangeability of cards between the two platforms is problematic.

■ DIGITAL AUDIO WORKSTATIONS

Before looking at a typical digital editing session, let's discuss the hardware that may be found in a typical DAW. Figure 6.3 shows a drawing of such a system. The basic computer is shown at point a. A power supply converts the input line AC current to the DC power required by the computer's components. The CPU chip, memory slots, and accessory slots are also shown. The interface accessory slots could be PCI,

ISA, VLB, or NuBus, depending on the type of computer. The memory slots are also configured for the platform selected.

A brief word about memory. Most DAW systems require a minimum of 16MB of RAM, which is the memory that comes on a SIMM or DIMM. Most modern computers have four slots. A SIMM is available in configurations of 4, 8, 16, 32, 64, and 256MB. Usually, memory SIMMs must be installed in pairs, that is, two 8MB or four 4MB SIMMS for 16MB of RAM. You can never really have too much memory. Although 16MB may be the minimum requirement, substantial improvement in performance can be realized by upgrading to 32, 64, or even 128MB. Most DAW cards contain their own DSP chips, but the computer CPU is still used for some computations and especially for the GUI screen refresh and redraw.

As seen at point c in figure 6.3, the DAW card fits into one of the slots in the computer and draws its power from the host computer system. The card contains the DAW manufacturer's DSP chips and additional memory as required by the system. On the end of the card are the interconnections that allow the card to address the outside world. These connections may be AES/EBU IOs (inputs/outputs) or propri-

Figure 6.3   Diagram of a computer-based digital audio workstation.

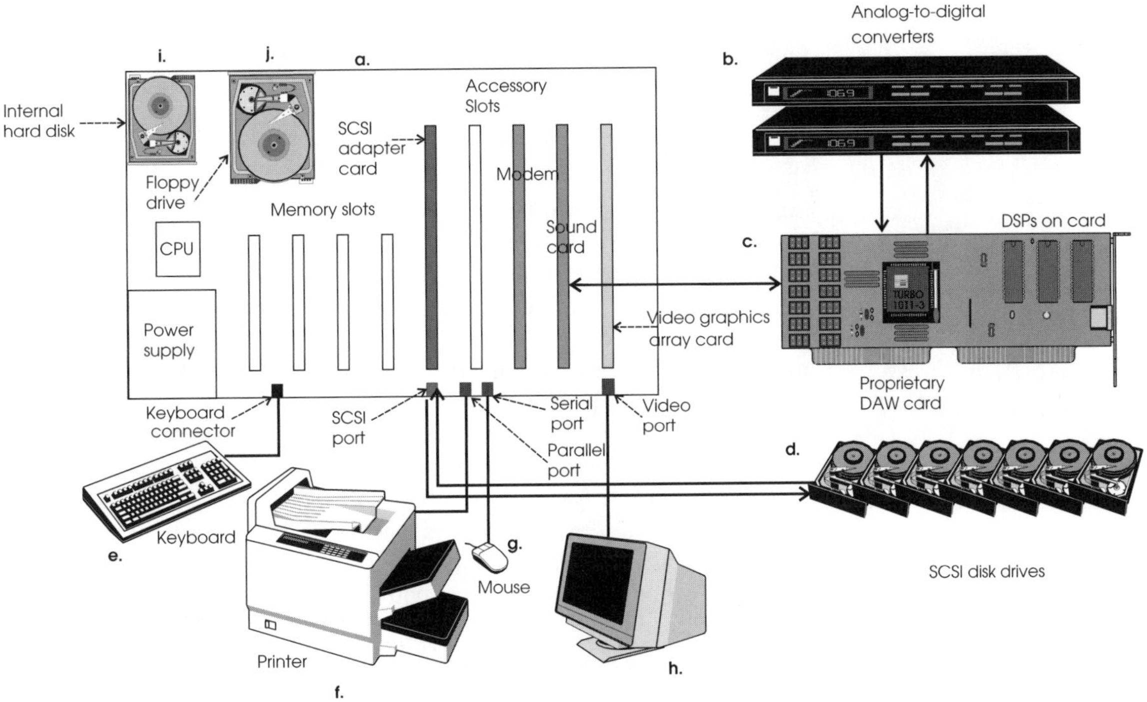

etary cable system connectors. These connections may be electrical wire conductors or fiber optic cables utilizing Toslink or other optic plugs, or they may be jacks for connecting to the outboard analog-to-digital and digital-to-analog systems. A second card may connect to the main card by an internal ribbon cable, requiring one slot for interface to the manufacturer's proprietary multichannel interface. Figure 6.4 shows a proprietary DAW card for use in a host computer.

Point b in figure 6.3 shows the outboard analog-to-digital converters that send and receive data back and forth between the card. These outboard converters connect to the external analog systems, such as mixers, tape recorders, or amplifiers and loudspeakers. Some manufacturers use proprietary converter devices that are specifically for their DAW system, whereas others leave the choice of converter to the user. It is possible in many cases to use only an outboard digital audio recorder containing its own converters. The recorder is connected to the DAW through either the AES/EBU or the S/PDIF ports. The possibilities for interconnection are equaled only by the number of DAW and sound card manufacturers.

Point d in figure 6.3 shows the outboard SCSI disks. As mentioned earlier, up to seven SCSI devices may be attached to the SCSI chain. Sometimes the SCSI devices are attached to a separate SCSI adapter that is supplied by the DAW manufacturer. In other cases the SCSI devices attach directly to SCSI connector on the DAW card. In some cases these SCSI disks do not appear on the computer desktop. In fact, some systems require special formatting for the SCSI drives that precludes the drives being used for anything but digital audio storage. Most PC systems use the new, faster SCSI-2 standard with the 50-pin plug instead of the original 25-pin SCSI configuration. Some of the older Apple Macintosh family of computers use a special circular SCSI connector.

Points e, f, and g in figure 6.3 show where the normal computer peripherals are attached. Many systems serve double duty and, when they are not being used as digital workstations for editing or mixing audio, often are used to do billing and inventory duties. Devices such as printers, plotters, scanners, and so on are often attached to the system. In many cases, track sheets, printed edit lists, and other information generated by the DAW software can be output in printed form for storage with the master audio material. The keyboard and mouse (points e and g) are standard input devices and are used to enter the user's instructions to the system. Trackballs and other pointing devices can be substituted for the mouse.

Point g in figure 6.3 shows a video monitor attached to the system through a VGA (video graphics array) accessory interface card. A small monitor presents problems when used with DAWs because

Figure 6.4   A DAW card for an ISA slot in a personal computer (photo courtesy Spectral Inc.).

of the large amount of information on the screen. Therefore, a minimum screen size of 17 inches is required. The larger the monitor, the less zooming in and out is required during the edit session. As mentioned earlier, most of the audio processing is done by the specialized DAW card. The system may make use of the host computer's math co-processor, but most of the number crunching goes on in the DSP chips. However, in most cases the host computer is used for the visual part of the system. Digital audio workstations place extreme requirements on the screen graphics part of the system because the data are complex. Changes to complex waveforms often require a very fast screen redraw. Waiting for the screen to refresh after moving a waveform by less than 10 milliseconds can be frustrating, and moving a chunk of audio from one location to another can be very difficult if the chunk continually lags behind the cursor. For these reasons the user should purchase the best video card possible for the host computer. The ISA cards in the PC are usually unacceptable because they are 16-bit cards. Older Macintoshes can be problematic, and although many of these systems have their video interfaces built into the motherboard, a faster accessory video card is usually necessary. The standard resolution of 640 × 480 (pixels) is seldom satisfactory, and resolutions of 800 × 600 or greater are usually necessary to fit the entire edit display on the screen in a readable form. Some systems require even higher resolutions.

Points i and j in figure 6.3 show the host computer system's internal disk drives. The hard drive, often called the *boot drive,* holds the DAW software. The floppy drive, usually a 3 ½-inch micro floppy disk drive, is used to load the software and updates. The programs often come on these 3 ½-inch disks but may come on a CD-ROM. The user installs the program onto the hard disk. Many manufacturers today put their software upgrades on computer BBSs (bulletin board systems) or on an Internet web page. The user simply downloads the material (often compressed or "zipped") through a modem or LAN (Local Area Network) connection.

Figure 6.5a shows an eight channel interface from a computer-based DAW. Figure 6.5b shows the rear of the interface, where the analog and digital inputs and outputs can be seen.

In the next chapter we examine in detail a simple two-channel editing session and a more complex multichannel edit-and-mix session.

Figure 6.5   a. An eight-channel digital I/O interface that includes digital-to-analog and analog-to-digital converters; b. the rear of the same interface showing the analog and digital and proprietary interface cable connections (photos courtesy Spectral Inc.).

a.

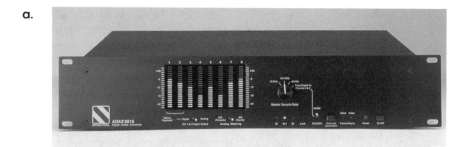

b.

SEVEN

The Digital Editing and Mastering Session

Assume that your digital audio workstation (DAW) is set up and ready to go. The cards have been installed, the software has been loaded, and the drives have been formatted and connected. The inputs and outputs of the analog-to-digital and digital-to-analog converters are connected to a small console where a DAT machine is patched in (i.e., connected through a patch bay with plug-in patch cables). Audio monitoring can be accomplished using headphones or loudspeakers, and your system features a 17-inch video monitor with a fast video card. Your client has brought a DAT tape with 20 minutes of digital audio that has been recorded in about 18 or 19 takes over a 2-day period. There is a marked score (music with the desired edits marked), and the client needs an edited two-track master DAT. Total time of the rough master DAT is 55 minutes.

The first step is to copy the material into the DAW, and at this point you need to make a decision on how to proceed with the editing. The two basic methods of editing are the assemble method and the insert-cut method. In the assemble method you select the first section of data that you wish to use, then move or copy the data to a new location. A second section of data is then selected and pasted to the end of the first section. The session proceeds this way, assembling each section of the music one after another. In the insert-cut method the music data are copied into the system in the desired order, and the spaces between the wanted musical sections are then cut out and discarded. This works well if all the musical material is recorded in sequential order. However, say that part of take 6 is needed to start the piece and that then you would need to jump back to take 3 for the middle section. Therefore, in this case the assemble process may be the easier of the two methods. Some engineers prefer to sequence the material as it is recorded into the DAW and include short pauses of a second or two between the sections. This makes it easy to identify the start and stop points of each section on the screen.

Figures 7.1, 7.2, and 7.3 show edit screens from three different editing systems. The number of panels in each figure differs, but note that the waveforms look similar. The vertical lines in the panels denote edits that have been made or are about to be made. Figure 7.1 shows a PC-based system where all the commands, including the transport controls, are on-screen buttons that are clicked on by the mouse or other pointing device. Four panels are shown. A system of this type truly requires a 17-inch monitor for the details on the screen to be legible.

Figure 7.1   Editing screen from Producer software by Spectral Inc.

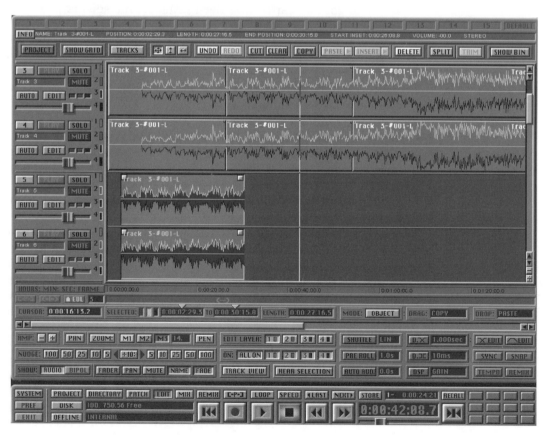

Figure 7.2   Editing screen from Session8PC software by DigiDesign (courtesy DigiDesign).

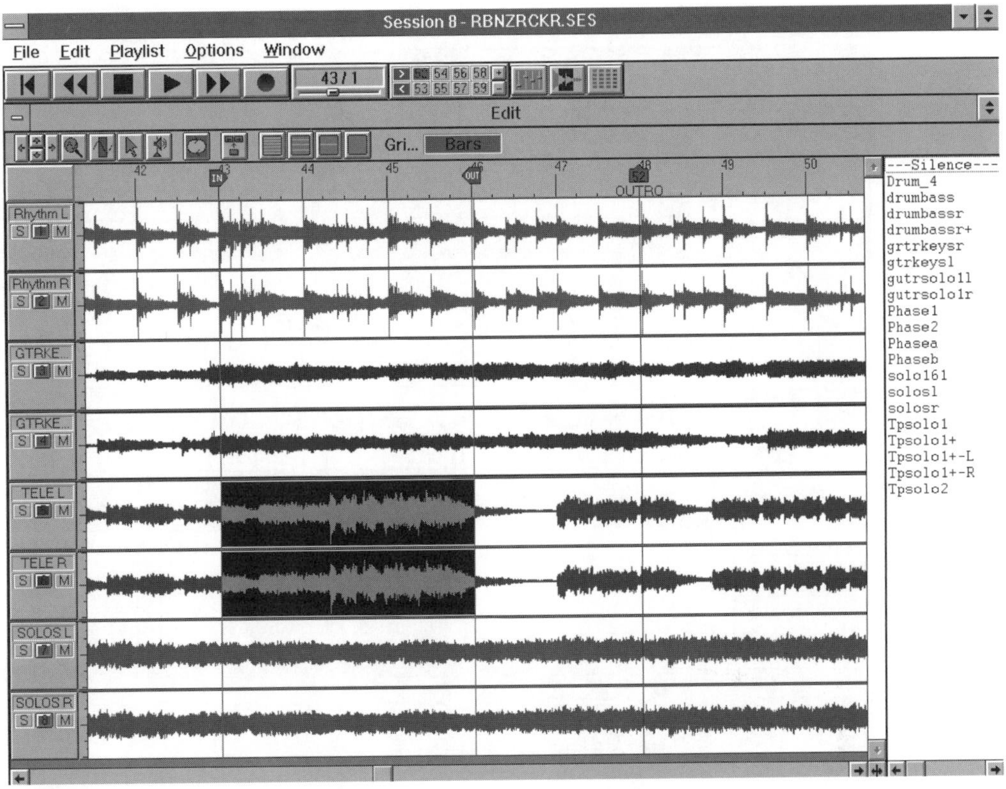

Figure 7.2 shows a screen with eight panels, all containing data. This menu-driven system is available as either a Macintosh- or as a PC-based system. The user selects a menu from the top bar, then a list of command options drops down from that location. Some options, as well as the transport controls, are available also as point-and-click command buttons. Note that at the top of the eight panels, in and out points are designated, although only the data on panels 5 and 6 have been selected. Figure 7.2 also shows a bin (or parking lot) on the right side of the screen to store data that are currently unused but that may be used later. In figure 7.1 the bins are the numbered boxes at the top of the screen. These bins are not really where the data are stored; rather, they are labeled pointers that access where the actual data reside on the hard drive. As mentioned earlier, in most systems the actual digital audio storage file is left untouched, and the edit process builds an EDL that references

Figure 7.3 Editing screen from Sonic Station software by Sonic Solutions (courtesy Sonic Solutions).

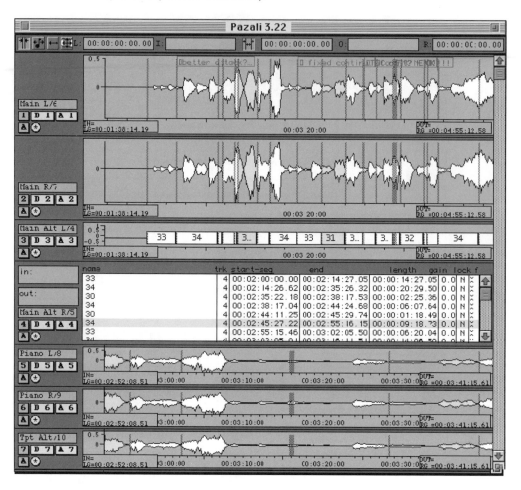

the original data and stores a set of commands telling the system where to start and stop playback. Because the access time of most hard-disk systems is about 12 milliseconds or less, the transitions are nearly instantaneous and therefore inaudible. Later in this chapter we discuss how this transition is handled by the system when a cross-fade is involved.

Figure 7.3 shows a Macintosh-based editing screen with seven panels visible. Panels 1, 2, 5, 6, and 7 show the graphical representation of the audio waveform, whereas panels 4 and 5 show the audio data in block form and text form, respectively. Note in these two panels that the data are not in sequential order as originally recorded into the system. The system shown in figure 7.3 is principally menu based, although this screen shot does not show the menu bar that is located at the top of the screen.

■ TRACKS, INPUT/OUTPUT CHANNELS, AND PANELS

On conventional reel-to-reel multitrack tape recorders, the data, whether digital or analog, are stored on tracks, which are longitudinal paths on the tape. Even helical scan devices such as DAT and videotape recorders call their data stripes tracks. This convention has carried through to the DAW jargon, and the panels on the screen are generally called tracks even though they are simply graphical representations of the digital audio that is stored at various locations on the hard disk. This is not to be confused with the number of individual input and output channels that a system can have.

Tracks can be real or virtual. Real tracks are assigned to specific outputs or inputs of the system. Systems may be able to display or store up to 99 virtual tracks or more, but unless the system has 99 physical input/outputs, all these tracks cannot be output or recorded simultaneously. In general, a set of analog-to-digital and digital-to-analog converters is required for each input and output channel. Systems may specify that they support 99 virtual tracks but may be capable of playing or recording only 16, 8, or even 4 at a time. Some of the less expensive systems that are based on the internal sound card of the PC or Mac can handle only two tracks at a time. Many systems allow internal mixing of virtual tracks for output to specific hardware channels. A typical internal mixer, shown in figure 7.4, allows playback and mixing of eight tracks to a stereo output. The track assignment and routing are assigned in a patch, or assignment, screen (which will be shown later in this chapter in the discussion of multitrack recording onto hard disk). However, each input strip can be assigned to any of the virtual tracks, and each channel strip contains auxiliary sends, equalization, filtering, automation control, panning, and level. Here you can also dictate whether the channel, and corresponding numbered track, is in play, record, or punch-in mode. The two-channel output section contains the master faders as well as the master auxiliary send level controls, the auxiliary returns, and some automation features. Note that the transport part of the screen is the same as that of the edit screen in figure 7.1.

Figure 7.4   Mixing panel screen from Producer software by Spectral Inc.

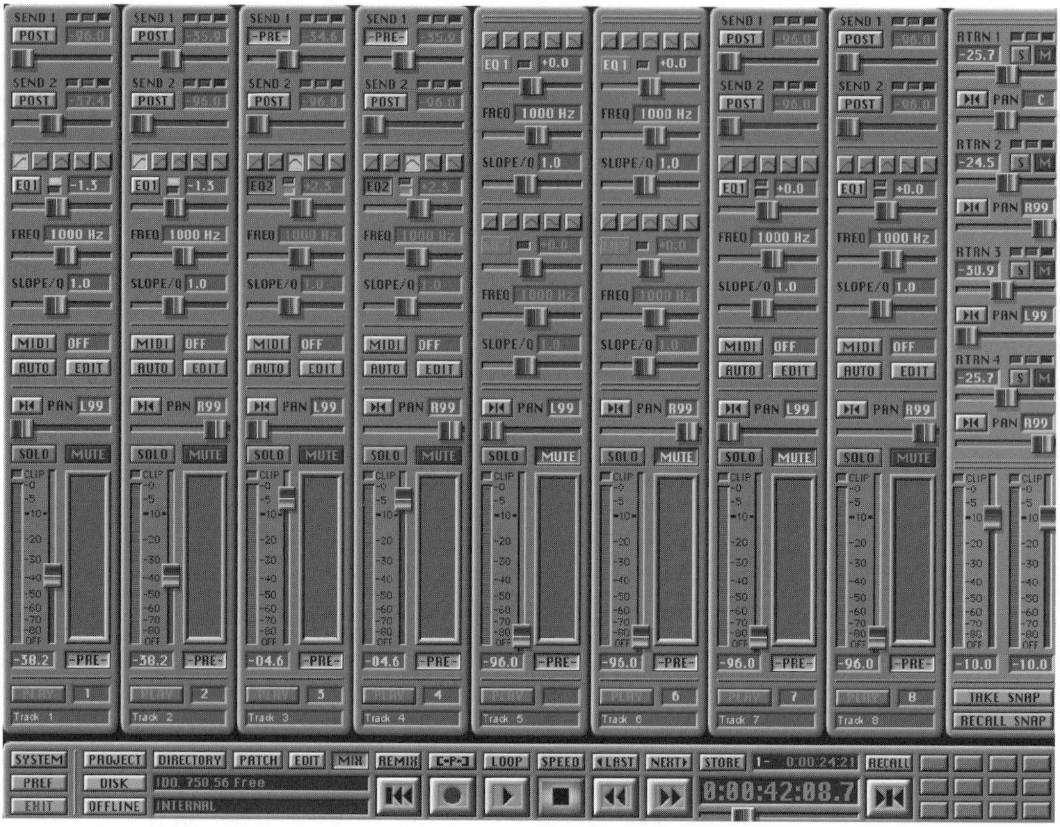

■ THE EDITING SESSION

Let's say that we have decided to copy the material as it was brought to us into the system and to use the assemble method of editing. This will be a two-track editing session, as the material was previously mixed down to two from, for example, a digital multi-track. All equalization and other effects have already been accomplished, and the levels are consistent from take to take. It is important to note that the prudent recording engineer will take care that levels from session to session on the same project are consistent. It is possible to match, for example, Tuesday's levels with Monday's levels after the fact, and most DAWs have the ability to change levels on a selected section, but it can be time consuming and may require long periods of trial and error.

You first open an edit screen and load the project into it or conversely, in some systems, load the project first and then open the edit screen. At this point it is probably best to reduce the number of panels or tracks that are displayed on the screen for easiest visibility. Only four panels are needed: two containing the original musical data and two empty ones where the edited master will be assembled. These are often called the *source panel* and the *destination panel,* respectively. Figure 7.5 shows this type of arrangement.

A brief aside on sample rates. Projects for CD must have a sample rate of 44.1kHz. Music for other media may use other rates (e.g., 48kHz or even 32kHz). It is imperative that all takes for a given edit project use the same sample rate, whatever it is. Although on many systems it is possible to edit together two sections of differing sample rates, an audible pitch shift will occur at the edit point when the selection is played in its entirety. If all elements of the project do not use the same sample rate or if the edited project is destined for CD and is not at a sample rate of 44.1kHz, a sample rate conversion is required. Sample

Figure 7.5   A portion of an editing screen showing the source and destination panels used during assemble editing.

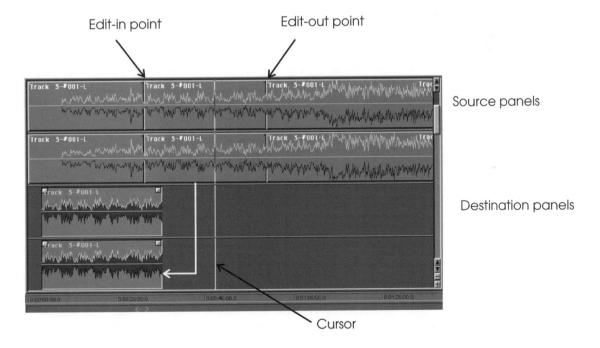

rate conversion is accomplished in most DAWs by interpolation and decimation, whereby the original signal is resampled at a very high rate, low-pass filtered at the new Nyquist frequency, and then mapped down to the new sample rate. This process is often not possible in real time and may take as much as three or four times the time span of the original selection. It may be better to edit, for example, a digital multi-track mixdown that was sampled at 48kHz and then downsample or decimate the entire edited project rather than to convert the sample rate of all the takes individually prior to editing.

It is always best to plan for a certain amount of time (e.g., 4 seconds) before the piece actually starts. Therefore, it is important to set the first edit-in point in the destination panels at that point. In fact, depending on what your postedit storage medium is, you may wish to start your project with 30 seconds of 1kHz tone followed by 30 seconds of digital silence, or so-called digital black. Different mastering media formats have different specifications. You may wish to check with the intended pressing plant or mastering facility before beginning your edits. At this point, because the whole 55 minutes of music is now contained in the top two panels, you must find the starting point for the beginning of the piece from, for example, take 4. This is where it is important to have a take sheet from the actual recording session. Nothing is more frustrating to the edit or mastering engineer than not knowing where on the session master the wanted material starts. The proper take sheet will list the length of each take and whether it is acceptable and complete as well as the start and stop time for that selection. Because the whole visual display of the piece is spread over about 7 inches (assuming a 17-inch monitor) on your screen, it may be difficult to locate where take 4 begins. However, after consulting the take sheet you find that take 4 starts at 6 minutes and 32 seconds into the session. At the top or bottom of the edit panels is a time line that may be calibrated in minutes, seconds, and tenths of seconds or in SMPTE time code (minutes, seconds, and frames), or, for film, in feet and frames. Usually, the time measurement increments are user selectable.

After locating the start point on the time line, you will see that the data (as shown in figure 7.6a) are a very dense waveform and that it is difficult to distinguish between the start of the take and the slate or end of the preceding selection. All DAWs have a zoom feature that may take the form of a wire-frame drawing tool, a hot key that zooms into the cursor position, or some other way of determining the position and size of the area to be displayed. Often the size of the zoom area can be preset in the preferences section of the software. The preference section is where the user defines the parameters such as the default sample rate and zoom amount that apply when

Figure 7.6   An edit panel showing a. normal resolution, b. expanded resolution, and c. resolution at the waveform level.

a.
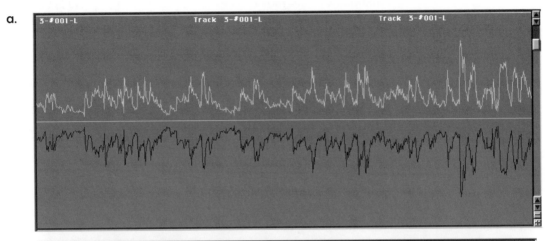

b.
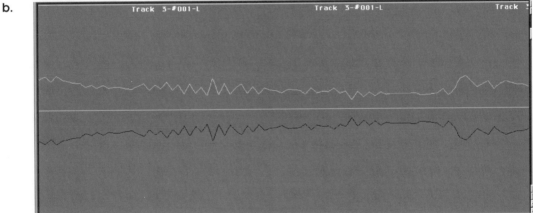

c.
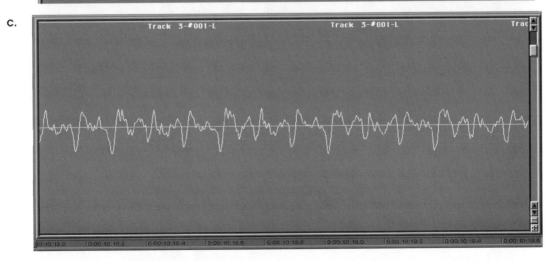

the software is first opened on the desktop. Figure 7.6b shows a section of the waveform after zooming in on the highlighted section. At this point the cursor can easily be placed at the precise beginning of the sound selection. It is possible to zoom in to the actual waveform for extremely precise cursor placement, as shown in figure 7.6c. After the cursor is set, it is wise to listen to the selection from that point to make sure that none of the sound has been accidentally cut off or that a portion of the take slate has not been included.

After it is determined that the cursor is in the correct place, an edit-in point or selection beginning marker of some kind is set in place. Now we can either play the selection up to the point where we wish to jump to the next good take or skip ahead to the selection end point, zoom in, and set the end selection mark or edit-out point. These marks, or edit points, may have different names depending on the manufacturer of the software, but they are used to define the in and out points and separate the desired portion of the sound from the undesired part.

Now, with either a copy-and-paste command or a cut-and-paste command, the designated area is taken from the source panels and placed in the destination panels at the designated start point. Some systems simply allow you to drag and drop the selected segments to the proper destination panels. Editing in stereo requires that both channels be edited together. If they are not, misalignment could occur, and the left channel may slightly lead or lag the right channel, causing timing alignment problems that can create phase anomalies on common material. This may not even be visible, but a lead or lag time of only 2 or 3 milliseconds can cause high-frequency phase cancellation when channels are played together. This synchronization will occur automatically in the so-called stereo mode, where the tracks have been linked as a stereo pair prior to editing. The editing engineer then turns his attention back to the source tracks or panels and sets the edit-in and edit-out points for the next part of the musical selection. Then the second section is placed in the destination panels also but is snugly butted up to the end of the first section. This process continues until the complete selection has been assembled. As can be seen in figure 7.3, a vertical line in each of the top two panels indicates where the sections were edited together.

Manipulation of the Edit Point

It is a good idea to listen to the portion of the song or selection where the edit has just occurred, and in many cases the default cross-fade will provide satisfactory results. The default cross-fade is usually set in the preferences menu of the software, allowing the user to determine the amount of time, in milliseconds, that is desired. You might recall in our discussion of tape-based digital editing that the edit point and cross-fade times could be adjusted by ear by manipulating the data in the edit buffer. The cross-fade at the edit point is also very similar to the cross-fading that occurs when overdubbing and/or punching in on the digital multitrack tape recorder (discussed in chapter 4). At the appropriate time, the end of the preceding section fades out as the beginning of the succeeding section fades in. This is shown in figure 7.7.

Sometimes, however, the edit just does not work the way the engineer intended. Levels may be slightly different, there may be a minor pitch discrepancy, or the waveforms will not quite mesh, such as when trying to edit in the middle of a sustained instrumental note when there is a prevalent vibrato. There are two options in most digital editing systems that can be of great help in this situation. First, the edit can be undone and tried again at a slightly different point. Most systems have an undo button or menu command with at least one level of undo; other systems have several levels of undo, some as many as 99. However, any number beyond 10 may require too much of the computer's resources of memory or disk space to be practical. The number of undo levels available is usually determined in the preferences setting. The undo action simply reverts the edit process to the state prior to the last action. So, if an edit was done, and it just does not "sound right," you can undo the edit, reset the edit points and assemble the edit again. Just try doing

Figure 7.7   The cross-fade and –3dB down point of a digital edit.

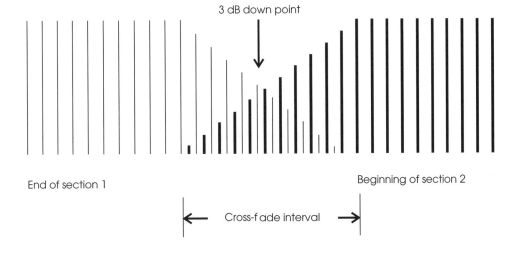

that with a razor blade and a piece of analog tape! Even tape-based digital editors allow you one level of undo, but the process of redoing the edit is as time consuming as the original edit. With the DAW system, edit points can be moved in small increments in either direction by using the cursor keys. Then the edit can be tried again.

However, now consider a situation where the spot for the edit cannot be changed yet the edit has an annoying glitch or pop. Here is where the edit cross-fade screen or "edit editor" is extremely handy. Figure 7.8 shows an edit cross-fade screen from a Macintosh-based DAW. The top panel displays the fade-out and the lower panel the fade-in. Although there is only one in and one out point, they represent the cross-fade in however many panels or tracks are selected on the edit screen. One of the most useful functions found in this section of the editor is the ability to change the slope of the cross-fade. Traditionally, with razor blade editing, the cross-fade slope is linear, as shown in figure 7.9. The cut angle is usually 45 degrees for full-track tapes and 30 degrees for two-track tapes. Multitrack tapes use angles between 9 and 30 degrees. However, with a digital editor you can change not only the "angle" of the edit by changing the length of the fade-out and fade-in but also the type of edit slope used. Some of the choices found in most DAW editors are linear, cosine, root-cosine, exponential, and alpha-exponential. Figure 7.8 shows a root-cosine in the upper fade-out panel and an alpha-exponential in the lower fade-in panel. Note the difference between the fade-in length, which is about 6.5 frames long, and the fade-out length, which is about 11 frames long. The time scale here is in SMPTE time code, so 00:03:16:15 is 3 minutes, 16 seconds, and 15 frames, where a frame is equal to $\frac{1}{30}$ of a second. Here you can also listen to either the fade-in or the fade-out to see whether any unwanted sound is included at the edit point. If there is an undesirable sound, the point can be shifted in either direction by very small amounts with the nudge buttons. Here the nudges are set up for 10 frames ($\frac{1}{3}$ of a second), 20 frames ($\frac{2}{3}$ of a second), or 1 second. This particular system also allows you to set up edit templates so that after you have created the perfect edit configuration for the kind of musical production you are working on, you can store the characteristics in a template file. Then the template can be called up when desired and applied to any other edit point. Your perfect edit template can also be stored as the default edit so that any time you make a splice, the template is applied.

Figure 7.10 shows a different type of edit adjuster. Here you can type in a value or use a mouse-activated slider to adjust the length of the edit as well as the length of the fade-in and fade-out. The slopes for both fade-ins and fade-outs can be selected by pointing and clicking on one of the slope buttons on either side of the screen. The buttons to the left select the fade-out slope and the buttons to

Figure 7.8   The Edit Cross-Fade screen from a Sonic Station (courtesy Sonic Solutions).

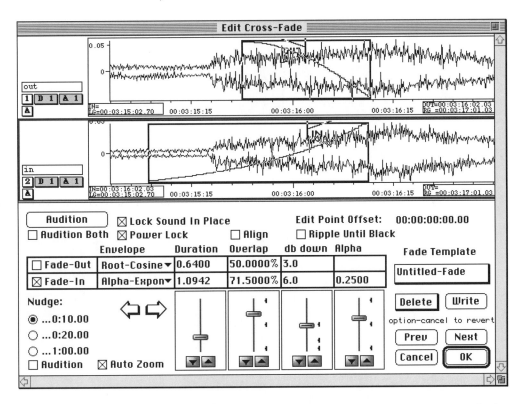

the right the fade-in slope. You can also use the mouse to grab the handles in the edit display window and move the edit point back and forth on the selected slopes. This can be done in real time while playing the edit or by looping the edit between two points set in the pre-roll and post-roll windows. Looping allows you to hear the edit changes as you adjust. Figure 7.11 shows the region being edited by the edit fade window of figure 7.10. The dark area in the center represents the amount of material common to both segments. Here also the edit can be adjusted by dragging, with the mouse or other pointing device, one side of the edit or the other to lengthen or shorten the amount of material included in the overlap.

After all the edits have been completed, the project may require some mastering, or so-called CD preparation. This is where the P and Q subcodes (discussed in chapter 5) are inserted either within the selection in a multimovement piece or at the beginning of the selection of a single, continuous piece. These codes mark where the track starts, its timing, the track number, and other information

Figure 7.9   A magnetic tape splice with a linear slope.

Magnetic tape

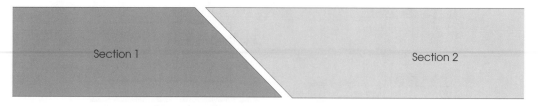

45-degree cut

Figure 7.10   a. The fade-in, fade-out editor; b. the cross-fade editor from Producer software by Spectral Inc.

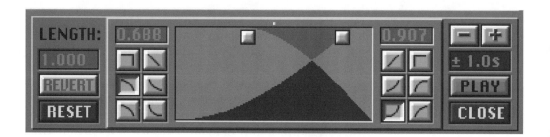

used by the CD player for proper playback. Some DAW editing systems include this capability, whereas others do not.

The session ends when all the desired musical segments have been assembled in the proper order. At this point the EDL is saved and the entire piece played while the engineer and producer follow the score to make sure that none of the edits are incorrect or audible. Then the selection is usually output to another storage medium, such as DAT, Exabyte, or CD-R, for either archival use or delivery to the client.

Figure 7.11   The selected edit area.

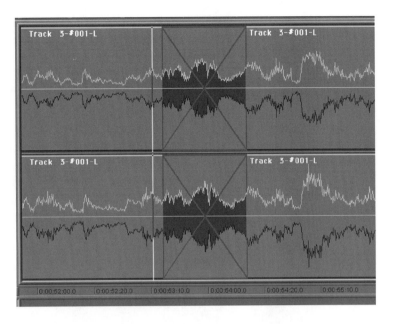

■ THE MULTITRACK HARD-DISK RECORDING SESSION

The process of recording multitrack to hard disk is not at all unlike the reel-to-reel multitrack process. The first step is to decide which basic tracks are to be recorded first and where they should be assigned. In many cases, the outputs of the recording mixer are assigned sequentially to the tracks on the recorder. Or, if the DAW's internal mixer is to be used, the output of the microphone preamplifiers delivers a line-level signal directly to the multichannel analog-to-digital converter. If these sequential channel assignments are not correct for the current project, the user can either change the cabling or reassign the inputs to tracks in the DAW patch screen. A patch screen of a DAW is shown in figure 7.12. Note that the physical inputs are numbered across the top of the screen and the virtual inputs, or tracks, down the right side. Note also that the left and right master virtual outs are patched to the main physical outs, which are probably hardwired to a DAT or other outboard storage device. In this example, there is an 8-channel I/O device assigned to the first 8 virtual tracks. Some systems have physical inputs of up to 32 or more, whereas smaller systems may only have 8 physical channels. Regardless, most systems allow a nearly unlimited number of virtual tracks so that after the first 8 parts are recorded, an additional 8 can be added to tracks 9 to 16, then 17 to 24, and so on until the system runs out of disk space. Figure 7.13 shows an 8-I/O system with 16 tracks of information recorded.

Let's say that we first want to record four tracks of rhythm instruments. The output of the mixer or microphone preamplifiers are fed to the first four tracks of the DAW. In some cases the levels are set at the mixer or preamplifiers, and in others the input gain can be set by the DAW's internal mixer, as shown in figure 7.4. In either case, the tracks are armed for recording, or put in the "ready" mode. The DAW starts recording, and the instruments begin to play. After the perfor-

Figure 7.12   A DAW software patch screen from Producer software by Spectral Inc.

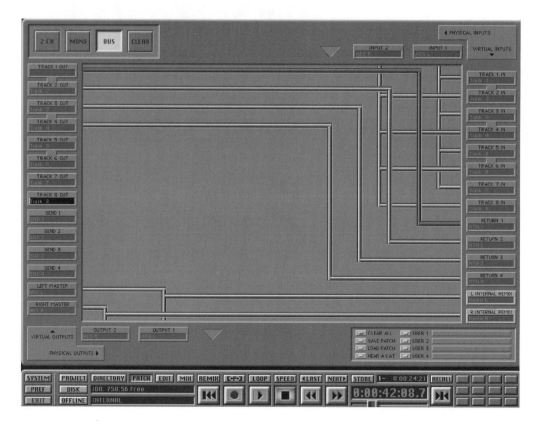

mance the operator hits the stop button, and the data appear on the edit screen. If the take is good, more parts are added; however, if the take is not good, the entire section can be played and recorded again onto the same tracks with the new data replacing the original.

However, let's say that all parts of the performance are good except for four or five bars in one instrumental part. In the traditional multitrack world, the tape would be rewound and the offending bars replaced by "punching in" the new data. That is, the tape recorder would place the problem tracks in playback while the performer listens on headphones. When the punch-in point is reached, the recorder drops into record and replaces the original material with the new data. At the "punch-out" point, the tape recorder returns to the play mode. This is possible also in the DAW scenario. However, a better way may be for the player to simply to play the part again and have the engineer record it on another virtual track.

Figure 7.13   A 16-track edit screen from Producer software by Spectral Inc.

Then, when a version that suits everyone is done, the data can simply be cut and pasted into the original track. In fact, several takes of the basic tracks might be recorded onto various virtual tracks, after which a composite edit could be created bar by bar and track by track if necessary, thus creating a perfect set of rhythm tracks prior to adding additional parts.

Next, the other parts are added. The original tracks are put in the play, or "safe," mode and monitored while the other parts are recorded in synchronization with the original material. Here again, several takes of the additional parts can be recorded and a composite assembled to complement the original tracks.

When all tracks have been recorded, the selected tracks, in this case eight, are assigned to the internal mixer for playback mixing, equalization, and any other processing that may be desired. Note in figure 7.4 that tracks 1 to 8 are assigned to mixer channels 1 to 8. This need not be the case, however, as any tracks can be assigned to any mixer channel. If the mix is relatively static, that is, if a minimal amount of fader manipulation is required once the balance has been set, during playback the mix output is simply sent to the master outboard recorder. The output could also be sent, or "bounced," to an available set of internal tracks if editing of the two-channel mix is desired. However, if extensive fader movements during playback are required, the material can be mixed a few channels at a time and the fader moves stored until all channels have been processed in this way. Then during playback the onboard automation system controls the level of each channel on the basis of the previously stored data, and mixer two-channel output is sent out to the mastering DAT deck or CD-R. Some systems accomplish this automation using a linked MIDI sequencing program to control the fader and pan levels. Often, equalization changes and auxiliary sends can be automated as well.

Prior to the final mix, the equalization would have been adjusted, panning would have been established, and in the case of some systems, reverberation and other effects could have been added and automated if desired. Many of these so-called plug-ins are available as options for the DAW from the manufacturer or other outside vendors.

As you can see, it is possible in many cases for the DAW to take the place of the console, the tape recorder, the effects rack, and the edit system, thereby integrating the entire system into a complete, easy-to-use package. All the user needs to add is the monitoring hardware.

EIGHT

Signal Interconnection and Transmission

■ ELECTRICAL INTERCONNECTION

One of the great advantages of digital audio is the ability to clone data. Unlike the analog tape copy process, digital audio can be duplicated many times with no noticeable degradation. In the conventional analog scenario, the recording from, for example, tape recorder A is converted from magnetic energy to electrical energy and then sent along a cable to tape machine B, where it is reconverted to magnetic energy and stored on magnetic tape. As the recording is played back from the original magnetic tape and converted to electrical energy, noise comes with it. Tape asperity noise, wow and flutter from the analog transport, noise from the playback electronics and so on add to the signal that is being transferred. In addition, any electrical interference in the cable, impedance mismatches, and cable configuration problems can further degrade the signal. The signal is then subjected to another conversion (this time back to magnetic energy) and stored on tape with any additional noise created by the record electronics and the record transport wow and flutter and other distortions. At best, the copied signal has only 3dB or 4dB less signal-to-noise ratio than the original. However, distortions in the frequency response often occur as well.

The digital advantage is that data can be transferred from one source to another without leaving the digital domain. We can simply send the digital audio bit stream down a cable or through the air, after which it can be converted back to analog at the receiving end or simply recovered as a clone of the original data. Early in the development of digital audio it was recognized that standard protocols for transferring digital information were needed.

SDIF-2 Interconnections

The Sony Digital Interface Format was one of the earliest protocols developed. (An earlier system, called SDIF, was discarded when the SDIF-2 system was adopted.) The SDIF-2 was developed by Sony for data transfers between CD mastering machines. Recall from chapter 4 that the Sony PCM-1630 system and its predecessors (the PCM-1600 and PCM-1610) were designated by Sony and Philips as the mastering system for the CD. The system uses a separate cable for each channel of data along with a separate synchronization (or clock) signal. Therefore, on the connection panel of a PCM-1630 system are two data inputs and two data outputs with a word clock input and output, totaling of six connections using BNC connectors on coaxial cable. Some newer versions provide all these signals on a special eight-pin connector, sometimes called a *composite digital connector*. The signals are sent serially as 32-bit packets containing 29 data bits; the remaining 3 bits are used for synchronization. The system is capable of 20-bit quantization, and the first 20 bits are used for the digital audio signal. If 16-bit audio is being used, the remaining 4 bits are zeroes.

In addition to digital audio data, other pertinent subcode and identifying data are carried as well. Bits 26 and 27 tell the receiving system whether emphasis was used on the original recording. Recall from chapter 2 that emphasis was used in some systems to further raise the high frequencies above the quantization noise and to compensate for anti-aliasing filters that attenuated some high frequencies. Bit 28 is a copy-prohibit bit that, if set, will prohibit other machines using this protocol from going into record. (Copy prohibition is discussed later in this chapter.) Bit 29 signifies the beginning of the sync block, and bits 30 to 32 are the sync information.

AES/EBU Interconnections

As more manufacturers began establishing their own digital transfer protocols, the Audio Engineering Society established a standard transmission interface called the AES3 protocol, which was also accepted by the European Broadcast Union. This standard became known as the AES/EBU Digital Interface. Like the SDIF-2 system, the data are serial and include subcode information with the audio information. Unlike the SDIF-2, the AES/EBU system carries two channels on one balanced cable. A balanced cable is a three-conductor cable using an XLR, or so-called Canon connector. The IEC professional broadcast protocol (i.e., the IEC-958 Type I) is nearly identical to the AES/EBU standard. The system was designed to be used with existing professional cables that use a twisted pair and a shield or drain wire. Connectors are of the XLR type: pin 1 is the ground, and pins 2 and 3 carry between 3 and 10 volts peak to peak. The impedance of the system is low for both output and input. The AES/EBU specification calls for source and load impedance of 110 ohms over a frequency range of 100kHz to 6MHz. Although many installations have used standard microphone cable to carry the signal, it is highly recommended that special cable with a 110-ohm impedance be used to facilitate the best possible signal transfer. Also, unlike the SDIF-2 system (which is limited in cable length), the AES/EBU interface was designed to be successfully used with cable lengths up to 350 feet without equalization and can be extended further when equalization is used to compensate for high-frequency roll-off. The signal uses FM channel coding and is self-clocking so that it does not require a separate word clock connection. The data are coded into 32-bit subframes capable of up to 24-bit audio quantization. The remaining 8 bits are used to define audio channels (left and right), channel status, sync information, and user data. The channel status bit forms a block of data 192 bits long divided into 24 bytes. The first bit in byte 0 defines whether the remaining information conforms to professional or consumer channel status protocols. The professional mode can define emphasis status and type, copy-prohibit and -permitted status, sample rate and data reliability data, time of day, and other information (e.g., SMPTE time code).

MADI Interconnection

The AES/EBU digital transfer protocol is specifically designed for stereo or two-channel data transfer. A standard for multichannel digital transmission was developed by a consortium of manufacturers so that digital multichannel tape recorders could be digitally connected with digital recording consoles and other digital multitrack systems. The MADI (Multichannel Audio Digital Interface) system, also referred to as AES10, is very much like the AES/EBU code in format; however, 56 channels of data are multiplexed together for transfer on a single cable. The system uses a coaxial cable with BNC connectors and a sync cable that carries timing data. In the AES/EBU system the sample rate of the digital audio controls the data rate of the transmission channel. In the MADI system the rate is set to a constant 100MB per second, equivalent to a 20-bit signal at a rate of 50kHz. At rates lower than this, the extra bits are filled with zeroes. The only caveat is that all 56 channels must use the same sample rate. This is not an inconvenience, however, because all channels of a multitrack digital tape recorder are usually sampling at the same rate. The MADI system transfers all 56 channels of data sequentially, and 1 of the first 4 bits in each frame tells the system whether the channel is active and, in the case of a stereo pair, whether it is the left or the right channel.

S/PDIF Interconnection

The S/PDIF (Sony/Philips Digital Interface) was derived from the AES/EBU standard and shares many of its characteristics. However, the 192-bit channel status string is divided into 12 words, each comprising 2 bytes, or 16 bits. Early versions of the interface were incompatible with professional machines because the first bit in byte 0 was used to define four-channel status instead of whether the data were in the consumer or the professional format. However, when a new protocol (called IEC-958) was established, the multi-channel status data were moved, and bit 1 of byte 0 defined consumer or professional status, as it does in the AES/EBU protocol. The S/PDIF interface is now often correctly referred to as the IEC-958 Type II standard.

If the consumer status flag is set, it is followed by a category code that will define the type of equipment sending the bit stream. Categories for source machinery are defined (e.g., CD player, DAT machine, and external analog-to-digital converters) are defined. The list is open ended, and new categories continue to be added. For example, when the code defines a CD player, the subcode information from the disk is transferred also. When the code signifies DAT, start, skip, and stop IDs (along with other information pertinent to the DAT format) are transmitted. The S/PDIF (IEC-958 Type II) standard uses unbalanced audio cable consisting of only two wires with the negative tied to ground. It uses RCA-type phono plugs (also called cinch connectors) and has a peak signal value of ½ volt. It is recommended that 75-ohm video cable be used for maximum stability. Like the professional version, the channel status code conveys information regarding emphasis, channel data, copy-prohibit and -permitted status, sample rate, and other information. In addition, if the consumer flag is set, bit 15 defines the status of the Serial Copy Management System.

The Serial Copy Management System (SCMS) was developed to prevent unauthorized digital copies from being made. When consumer DAT machines were first imported, there was a fear that large-scale copying of pre-recorded digital material would occur, thereby depriving artists and songwriters of their legitimate royalties. An earlier system to prevent copying (called the CBS Copycode System) was tried, but it proved to be detrimental to the encoded music. The compromise was the SCMS, which allows digital copies to be made from a digital source. As the copy is made, however, the copy protection flag is set, and consumer digital recorders will not enter the record mode if this flag (bit 15) is sensed at the digital input. Therefore, the system allows copying from the source but will not allow a copy of a copy to be made.

■ OPTICAL INTERCONNECTION

All the interconnections between digital machines discussed so far are electrical. A limitation of electrical cabling is distance. As distance increases, so does cable capacitance and resistance which lead to frequency degradation. Electromagnetic interference and other induced noises are also a problem. In addition, grounding problems can occur when the transmitter and receiver are too far apart. One solution to this problem is the science of fiber optics, which, although relatively new, easily lends itself to the transmission of digital signals. Bandwidth is very wide, fiber optic cable is not susceptible to RFI (radio frequency interference), and grounding problems are nonexistent. Figure 8.1 lists frequencies found in everyday use. Note that higher frequencies approach the light spectrum.

The fiber optic range is just below the visible light spectrum. A small LED (light emitting diode) or laser generates light, which is then modulated by the signal being sent. A photoelectric cell on the other end converts the modulated light back to an electrical signal. Light follows the same rules for refraction and reflection as sound. Light is contained in the fiber by utilizing a principle called *total internal reflection* (TIR). In short, as long as the angle of reflection is kept above the critical angle, light will be guided through the fiber medium. The critical angle is a function of the density relationship between two media. The optical fiber consists of a core, a cladding and a buffer. The core carries the light signal, the cladding contains it, and the buffer protects the core and cladding.

Many signals can be sent along one cable. The signals are multiplexed at the transmitting end and are demultiplexed at the receiver.

Figure 8.1   Frequencies and their uses.

0Hz DC
1Hz–16Hz Low rumble
50Hz–60Hz AC voltage
16Hz–20Hz Range of hearing
10kHz–14kHz Radio navigation
14kHz–90kHz Marine mobile
90kHz–110kHz Radio navigation
110kHz–200kHz Marine mobile
200kHz–285kHz Air mobile
285kHz–415kHz Radio navigation
415kHz–490kHz Marine mobile
490kHz–535kHz Mobile
535kHz–1,605kHz AM broadcast
1,605kHz–1,800kHz Mobile
1,800kHz–2,000kHz Amateur
2MHz–3,35MHz Mobile
3.5MHz–4MHz Amateur
4MHz–5.95MHz Government
5.95MHz–6.2MHz Shortwave
6.2MHz–7MHz Government
7MHz–7.3MHz Amateur
7.3MHz–9.5MHz Government
9.5MHz–9.775MHz Shortwave
9.775MHz–11.7MHz Government
11.7MHz–11.975MHz Shortwave
11.975MHz–14MHz Government
14MHz–14.35MHz Amateur
14.35MHz–15.1MHz Government
15.1MHz–15.45MHz Shortwave
15.45MHz–17.7MHz Government
17.7MHz–17.9MHz Shortwave
17.9MHz–21MHz Government
21MHz–21.45MHz Amateur
21.45MHz–21.75MHz Shortwave
21.75MHz–25.6MHz Government
25.6MHz–26.1MHz Shortwave
26.1MHz–26.96MHz Mobile
26.96MHz–27.41MHz CB
27.41MHz–28MHz Mobile

28MHz–29.7MHz Amateur
29.7MHz–30MHz Mobile
30MHz–50MHz Government
0MHz–54MHz Amateur
4MHz–72MHz TV channels 2–4
2MHz–76MHz Air navigation
76MHz–88MHz TV channels 5–6
88MHz–108MHz FM broadcast
108MHz–118MHz Air navigation
118MHz–138MHz Aircraft voice
138MHz–144MHz Government
144MHz–148MHz Amateur
148MHz–164MHz Business/police
164MHz–174MHz Public service
174MHz–216MHz TV channels 7–13
216MHz–220MHz Radio location
220MHz–225MHz Amateur
225MHz–328MHz Government
328MHz–335MHz Air navigation
335MHz–400MHz Government
400MHz–420MHz Mobile
420MHz–450MHz Amateur
450MHz–470MHz Land mobile
470MHz–806MHz TV channels
14–83806MHz–960MHz Land mobile
960MHz–1215MHz Air navigation
1215GHz–1.3GHz Amateur
1.3GHz–300GHz Microwave, satellite, space
7.5×10^{10}Hz–4.0×10^{14}Hz Infrared light
4.0×10^{14}Hz–7.69×10^{14}Hz Visible light
7.69×10^{14}Hz–6.0×10^{16}Hz Ultraviolet light
6.0×10^{16}Hz–9.8×10^{19}Hz X rays

By wavelength
4,000µm–750nm Infrared light
1,600nm–850nm Fiber optic range
750nm–390nm Visible light
390nm–5nm Ultraviolet light

For digital audio, the signals can be AES/EBU protocol data, an S/PDIF-type signal, or other digital transfer format. Work is currently underway to create a MADI fiber optic protocol. Today, many consumer and some professional systems use the Toslink system (developed by Toshiba Electronics), which typically uses plastic fiber cable with an effective range of only about 50 feet. On the other hand, many professional systems use glass fiber cable, which can be extended to an indefinite length with the use of optical repeaters. A few disadvantages of fiber optic systems exist. One problem is that specialized tools and knowledge are required to splice, repair, or connect fiber cable. Even so, LANs (local area networks) of PC systems often run a fiber optic backbone between major locations that connect so-called hubs, where the signal is reconverted back to the electrical state for local distribution.

Other Digital Transmission Formats

Over the years, several other nonstandard digital transfer formats have evolved, including the ProDigi format, which is used between its recorder/players. However, this digital multitrack tape format has virtually disappeared and thus is of little consequence. Other obsolete interfaces include the Yamaha stereo interface and the IMS (Dyaxis I) stereo data transfer protocols.

The Tascam Digital Interface (TDIF-1) is essentially a multichannel S/PDIF connection. It uses a 25-pin sub-D connector on a single cable to carry digital data to and from the DA-98 digital modular multitrack recorders. Machine control data are also carried so that functions on the master machine will be echoed by the slave transports.

The Alesis Digital Interface (ADI) is an optical interface that carries all eight of the ADAT systems channels over one cable. It is designed to connect multiple ADAT recorders for digital audio signal transfer as well as for machine control of these devices. It can also transfer data between effects processors and DAWs that utilize the same protocol. Some digital consoles use this protocol as well.

■ DIGITAL AUDIO BROADCAST

No book on digital audio would be complete without some mention of digital audio broadcasting (DAB). Although this technology has been available for some time, very little movement has occurred other than in the cable television industry. Broadcasting has always been analog, and even when stations play CDs the transmitted signal is analog. Both AM and FM have problems with multipath distortion, limited bandwidth, limited dynamic range, stereo separation, and so on. Digital audio broadcast differs from AM and FM by modulating the phase of the carrier signal instead of the amplitude or the frequency.

We saw in figure 8.1 the extent of allocated frequencies. As more commercial services (e.g., mobile phone systems) require more frequencies, the limit of what can be accomplished on the airways will be reached. Digital audio broadcast can be the solution to a number of these problems. With data-reduction techniques an audio signal can be digitally encoded to require very little bandwidth when broadcast, thus freeing up some existing frequencies for other uses. An analog-to-digital converter is located at the transmitting station and a digital-to-analog converter in the listener's receiving device. In the case of digital media playback, such as from CD, the signal remains in the digital domain until reception. A number of stations (12 or more) could also share the same frequency allocation because several channels of material can be combined in one transmission. This is accomplished using multiplexing as well as time and frequency interleaving. The receiver will be able to determine the desired program and then demultiplex it from the others contained in the same carrier. Signals can be broadcast locally or sent to satellites for distribution. A sample rate of 32kHz has been selected for the DAB system, and emphasis can be used if desired because the receivers have the ability to read the emphasis flag in the bit stream. This provides a frequency response beyond that of the current FM systems, and signal-to-noise ratios can exceed 80dB through data reduction (as with the mini-disc system).

Although the United States has not implemented DAB, it is being tried on an experimental basis in Japan, and a system called NICAM is being used in Europe for digital stereo sound on television broadcasts. Some broadcasters today are sending multiple channels of digital audio to consumers over the cable television system. In such cases the listener rents or buys a digital decoder from the cable system and pays a monthly fee for the service. For this, 20 or more stereo program channels can be sent to the listener's hi-fi system. One cable company is providing 28 stereo signals with a frequency response of 10Hz to 16kHz and a dynamic range of 90dB. The decoder box may also have a S/PDIF digital output using either RCA or Toslink connectors. It remains to be seen whether DAB will become more commonplace.

Glossary

ABS—Absolute time. Time data that is recorded in the subcode on DAT and other digital recording media.

ADPCM—Adaptive Delta Pulse Code Modulation. A digital audio coding scheme that records the difference between successive samples. Used in CD-I.

AES—Audio Engineering Society.

AES/EBU—Digital audio transfer protocols established by the Audio Engineering Society and the International Broadcast Union.

Aliasing—Distortion that is caused when an analog-to-digital converter's sample rate is lower than twice the highest frequency that is to be recorded.

Amplitude—The maximum value of a waveform above its reference value.

Attenuation—Reduction in the amplitude of an audio signal.

ATF—Automatic Track Finding. The method used in azimuth recording to synchronize the transport with the tape. Used in place of control track signals.

ATRAC—Adaptive Transform Acoustic Coding. The data-reduction scheme used in the MiniDisc system.

Balanced Signals—A signal containing both a positively and a negatively moving waveform of equal amplitude (often referenced to ground). Necessary for common-mode rejection.

Bandwidth—The range, usually in hertz, between the high-frequency and low-frequency cutoff points in a system.

Baud Rate—The number of bits per second in a digital transmission line.

Bit—A BInary digiT. The smallest unit of digital information, usually consisting of a 1 or a 0. Eight bits make up 1 byte, and a series of bits make up a digital word.

CD—The audio-only compact disc. A digital storage medium that holds 660 MB of data, or 74 minutes of digital audio. Uses 16-bit linear PCM at a 44.1kHz sample rate.

CD+G—Compact Disc with graphics. Digital audio with still or motion pictures. Used in karaoke.

CD-I—Compact Disc Interactive. Digital audio with sound and pictures. Used in multimedia. Allows user control over sequence of events.

CD-R—Recordable Compact Disc. Known as WORM (write once, read many) discs. Once recorded and "fixed," these cannot be erased or re-recorded.

CD-ROM—Compact Disc read-only memory. Computer data on CD. Can also contain audio. Used extensively for computer games and mass information storage.

CD-RW—Compact Disc ReWritable. The erasable re-recordable CD. Uses phase-change technology.

CD-V—Compact Disc with video. Usually contains music videos followed by several audio-only songs.

Chase—A synchronization mode in which the slave machine follows the movements of the master machine.

CIRC—Cross-interleaved Reed-Solomon code. An error-correction/-protection code used in digital audio recording and storage systems.

CLV—Constant linear velocity. The speed of the disc varies so that data are presented to the pickup device at a constant speed even though the circumference of the desired data changes with position.

Common-mode noise—A signal (not part of the audio information) that is common to both sides of a balanced signal.

CMRR—Common-mode rejection ratio. A measurement of a system's ability to reject common-mode noise. Usually expressed in dB and defining the difference between the amount of common noise entering the system and of that leaving it.

CRC—Cyclic redundancy check code. A code used in the digital bit stream to recognize and correct errors induced by the storage medium.

CTL—Control track. Used on video recorders to synchronize the helical head with the recorded track on tape.

Curie point—The temperature at which magnetism dissipates on a specific material.

DASH—Digital audio stationary head. The predominant method of fixed-head digital recording.

DAT—Digital audiotape recorder. Also a tape medium for the DAT recorder.

DAW—Digital audio workstation. A computer containing software and hardware for storing, editing, and processing digital audio information.

dBfs—Decibel full scale. The unit used to define the amplitude value of a digital signal on a dBfs meter where zero equals all bits used.

DCC—Digital Compact Cassette. A consumer digital format that is compatible with the analog cassette.

Digital headroom—None when metered on a dBfs meter.

Distortion—An unwanted change to the waveform. An extraneous part of the signal.

Dither—A low level of noise added to digital recording or transmission media that is used to linearize digital audio and reduce noise from quantization. Usually an amount equaling one-half of the LSB (least significant bit).

DVD—The Digital Versatile Disc. A CD type that holds a great amount of data by decreasing the pit size and spacing. Capable of double-layer, double-sided data storage.

Dynamic Range—The distance, in dB, between the noise floor and the saturation or distortion point of the equipment or media. In digital equipment, it is the ratio of full-scale signal to broad-band noise (0–20kHz) measured with a −60dBfs signal. The S/(N+D) measured with a −60dBfs signal and a 20kHz low-pass filter.

EBU—European Broadcasting Union.

Emphasis—A high-frequency boost on record, requiring a matching frequency roll-off on playback, to maximize high-frequency signal-to-noise ratio in digital systems.

Equalization—The process of changing the frequency balance of the original waveform by boasting or cutting specific frequency bands.

Frame/field—In video systems, a frame is a complete picture. Two fields make up a frame.

Frequency—The number of times or cycles per second a periodic waveform repeats itself. Expressed in hertz (Hz).

FSK—Frequency shift keying. A method of encoding binary data for transmission on analog media.

Glass master—A glass plate etched with digital audio data used in DVD and CD manufacturing processes.

Harmonic distortion—The addition of unwanted harmonics to the original waveform by either the transmission system or the storage medium.

IEC-958—A standard for transmission of digital audio signals. Type I is the professional standard and Type II the consumer standard.

Interleaving—The method of encoding recording data so that it is not stored in sequence.

Jam sync—The method of generating new SMPTE time code on the basis of existing code.

Jitter—Timing errors in the digital audio transfer process.

LD—Laser Disc. A motion picture, stored as analog data, with digital audio format.

LTC—Longitudinal time code. Linearly recorded SMPTE time code.

Lock—When two or more processors are linked by running from a single clock.

MADI—Multichannel Audio Digital Interface. Allows the transmission of up to 56 digital channels of audio information on a single cable.

MD—MiniDisc. A recordable erasable optical digital audio format developed by Sony and using the ATRAC system of data reduction.

MIDI—Musical Instrument Digital Interface. The serial method of sending and storing synthesizer control data.

MO disc—Magneto-optical disc. An erasable recording and reproduction disk in which laser is used to heat the disc to the Curie point so that the magnetic polarity of individual bits can be changed for recording.

NTSC—National Television Standard Committee. A television standard used in North America and Japan using 525 lines of vertical resolution and 30 frames per second (black and white).

Off-line editing—Digital or video editing of a copy of a program and assembling a list of assemble or insert edits defined by SMPTE time code positions.

On-line editing—Editing material in real time.

Oversampling—Using a multiple of the original sample rate to output a digital bit stream.

PAL—Phase alternate line. The video broadcast standard for Europe and the rest of Asia consisting of 625 lines of vertical resolution and 25 frames per second.

PASC—Predictive Adaptive Sub-Band Coding. The data reduction system pioneered by Philips and used for the DCC.

PCM—Pulse code modulation. The most common method of encoding digital audio signals.

PD—ProDigi. A stationary-head multitrack digital audio recording system.

Period—The time it takes a sound wave to complete 1 cycle.

Phase—The relationship between the positive and negative voltages in an audio signal or the relationship between the compression and rarefaction of an acoustic wave.

Pit—The depression in the CD that represents a digital bit.

PQ subcode data—Data that represents data used when mastering a CD. A "P" indicates start and stop points, whereas "Q" is a multibit word containing song number, timing, and other pertinent information.

Pre-groove—A groove molded into the recordable CDs and DVDs as well as the MiniDisc to control laser tracking.

Polarity—The relationship of a positive terminal of a connector to the negative one. See Phase.

Quantization—The number of bits used to establish the voltage level of the signal to be digitized.

RAM—Random access memory. Integrated circuits that store data for brief periods of time.

R-DAT—Rotary head DAT recorder.

RMS amplitude—The average value of a signal. The root mean square is the average of the sum of the voltages squared over a given period of time.

ROM—Read-only memory. Digital storage that cannot be cleared or erased on integrated circuits or CDs.

Sample rate—The periodic rate at which the value of analog signal is measured by the analog-to-digital converter or the rate at which the digital word is sent to the Digital-to-analog converter.

SCMS—The Serial Copy Management System. The system for preventing a digital recorder from making copies from a copy of a digital source.

SCSI—Small Computer Systems Interface. A serial data connection between computer peripherals. Allows up to seven devices on one connection chain.

SDIF-2—Sony Digital Interface, type 2. An interconnection protocol system for digital audio data transfer in which the left and right channels of the stereo signal and the In and Out are carried in separate cables. Also needs a clock signal connection. Uses BNC video type connectors.

SECAM—A video broadcast standard used in France and Russia. Similar to the PAL system but not compatible.

SMPTE—Society of Motion Pictures and Television Engineers. The standardizing organization for time code and video-related issues.

S/N ratio—The ratio, in dB, between the noise floor of a system and its maximum output capabilities.

S/PDIF—Sony philips Digital Interface. A digital audio signal transfer protocol requiring an In and Out for a stereo digital signal using unbalanced cable and RCA-type connectors. See IEC-958.

Subcode—Data recorded along with the digital audio data that can define formats, P and Q codes, and so on in many digital audio mediums.

Time constant—The time, usually in microseconds, required for a voltage to travel through a reactive component such as a capacitor or an inductor.

TOC—Table of contents. The area on a CD that defines where specific data are stored.

Unbalanced Signal—A signal that contains an audio signal and a ground return (common-mode rejection is not possible).

Video-CD—A CD-ROM that stores video, mainly full-length feature films, using MPEG-2 data reduction.

VITC—Vertical interval time code. Time code that is recorded in the vertical interval of the video signal.

Word Clock—A timing pulse that tells the digital audio converter when to examine the next digital word.

WORM—Write Once, Read Many. A recordable magneto-optical disc that cannot be erased or re-recorded.

Suggested Reading

Baert, Luc, Luc Theunissen, and Guido Vergult, Sony Service Centre (Europe), ed. *Digital Audio and Compact Disc Technology.* 2nd ed. Oxford: Newnes, 1992.

Borwick, John, ed. *Sound Recording Practice.* 3rd ed. Oxford: Oxford University Press, 1987.

Craven, Gerzon, "Lossless Coding for Audio Discs." Journal of the Audio Engineering Society 44, no. 9 (September 1996): 706–20.

Guenette, David, and Parker, Dana. *CD, CD-ROM, CD-R, CD-RW, DVD, DVD-R, DVD-RAM: The Family Album.* Online. *http://www.onlineinc. com/emedia/AprEM/parker4.html.* Internet, June 4, 1997.

Hitachi Corporation. *Information Systems and Electronics.* Online. *http://www.hitachi.com/Pfinder/5014.html.* Internet, June 4, 1997.

Kefauver, Alan. *The Audio Recording Handbook.* Baltimore: MII Publishing, 1997.

Kefauver, Alan, and John Woram. *The New Recording Studio Handbook.* New York: ELAR Publishing, 1989.

Minasi, Mark. *PC Upgrade and Maintenance Guide.* 4th ed. San Francisco: Sybex, 1994.

Parker, Dana, and Robert Starrett. *CD-ROM Professional's CD-Recordable Handbook.* Wilton: Pemberton Press, 1996.

Philips Corporation. *DVD Standards.* Online. *http://www.sel.sony. com/SEL/consumer/DVD/specs.html.* Internet, June 4, 1997.

Pioneer Corporation. *An Introduction to DVD Recordable (DVD-R)*. Online. *http://www.km-philips.com/dvd/dst_01.html*. Internet, June 4, 1997.

Pohlmann, Ken. *Principles of Digital Audio*. 2nd ed. Indianapolis: Sams, 1989.

Pohlmann, Ken, ed. *Advanced Digital Audio*. Indianapolis: Sams, 1991.

Pohlmann, Ken. *The Compact Disc: A Handbook of Theory and Practice*. Madison, Wis: A-R Editions, 1989; 2nd ed. *The Compact Disc Handbook,* 1992.

Robinson, D., and Dadson, R. *British Journal of Applied Physics* 7 (1956).

Sony Corporation. *About DVD*. Online. *http://www.sel.sony.com.SEL/consumer/dvd/specs.html*. Internet, July 4, 1997.

Steiglitz, Ken. *A Digital Signal Processing Primer*. Menlo Park, Calif.: Addison-Wesley, 1996.

Strasser. *Thin Film Technology for Data Storage Disks*. Tape/Disk Business, February 1997.

Watkinson, John. *The Art of Digital Audio*. 2nd ed. Oxford: Focal Press, 1994.

Woudenberg, Eric. *The MiniDisc™ Community Page*. Online. *http://www.hip.atr.co.jp/~eaw/minidisc.html*. Internet, May 17, 1996.

Index